WHAT IS THE BIBLE AND WHO IS IT FOR?

A Book for Beginners, Skeptics, and Seekers

Emanuel Cleaver III

What Is the Bible and Who Is It For? A Book for Beginners, Skeptics, and Seekers

The General Board of Higher Education and Ministry leads and serves The United Methodist Church in the recruitment, preparation, nurture, education, and support of Christian leaders—lay and clergy—for the work of making disciples of Jesus Christ for the transformation of the world. Its vision is that a new generation of Christian leaders will commit boldly to Jesus Christ and be characterized by intellectual excellence, moral integrity, spiritual courage, and holiness of heart and life. The General Board of Higher Education and Ministry of The United Methodist Church serves as an advocate for the intellectual life of the church. The Board's mission embodies the Wesleyan tradition of commitment to the education of laypersons and ordained persons by providing access to higher education for all persons.

Wesley's Foundery Books is named for the abandoned foundery that early followers of John Wesley transformed, which later became the cradle of London's Methodist movement.

What Is the Bible and Who Is It For? A Book for Beginners, Skeptics, and Seekers

ISBN 978-1-945935-93-0

GBHEM Publishing is an affiliate member of the Association of University Presses.

Manufactured in the United States of America

Contents

Acknowledgments v

Introduction vii

I. What Is the Bible? 1
- Hard to Read? Hard to Understand? 1
- What Is the Word of God? 3
- Who Wrote the Bible? 7
- What Is the Bible? 9
- How Did We Get the Bible? 16
- How Do We Read the Bible in Context? 22

II. Why Is the Bible Important? 27
- What Is the Value of Scripture? 27
- Who Is the Bible For? 34
- Looking for Proof? 36
- Is the Bible Still Relevant? 38
- Why Does It Matter? 41
- What Counts as Essential? 42
- What Exactly Is the Bible? 48

III. Why Do We Need to Be Saved? 51
- Why Does God Want to Save Us? 52
- How Does God Save Us? 53

Who Is Jesus and How Does He Fit In? 55
Is Jesus Really Who He Says He Is? 55
Why Do We Need Jesus? 62

IV. How Should We Interpret the Bible? 67
Why So Many Translations? 68
What Are Some Methods for Interpreting the Bible? 69
What about Disturbing Passages of Scripture? 75
How Should We Read the Bible Today? 78
Where Is the Bible Trying to Take Us? 79

V. Helpful Tools 87
Some Key Biblical Principles 87
Idolatry and the Mistreatment of the Poor 96
Scripture within Scripture 100
Loving Like Jesus 103
The Bible Is Not All Facts, but It Is All Truth 104

VI. So What? 107
Jesus's Life, Ministry, and Resurrection 107
Putting What You Read into Practice 111
Reading the Bible for Personal Meaning 112
If We Have the Bible, Do We Still Need the Church? 114
How Church Helps Us Live Our Faith 117
Abusing the Bible 121
Wrapping It All Up 127

Study Questions 131

Endnotes 133

Acknowledgments

I want to thank my wife, Sharon, and my children, Emanuel IV, Isaac, and Alayna, for the inspiration they gave me to write this book. I also want to thank them for being patient with me as I spent hours working to make this happen.

Introduction

The purpose of this book is to help modern readers of the Bible gain a greater appreciation and understanding of this timeless classic. Whenever you mention the word "Bible," the overwhelming majority of people on earth know exactly what you are talking about, whether they believe in it or not. Unfortunately, many are unable to decipher much of its meaning. It is simply too confusing. Consequently, a lot of people who believe in the power of the Bible rely on pastors and professors to make sense of it for them. This is perhaps one of the reasons why so many Christians are biblically illiterate—meaning that people have access to the Bible but don't read it. Many don't know what's in it or they make assumptions about what it really says. Therefore, a lot of people who don't know what it says have based their understanding of God on what they've heard from others, whether it is correct or not.

There are many Christians who believe the Bible says things that are not even in the book at all. I've heard people say, "God helps those who help themselves," believing that they are quoting directly from the Bible, when in fact the Bible does not say that. In all actuality there are many who believe the Bible suggests the very opposite. God helping those who can't help themselves is something that we see over and over again. In the midst of pervasive obliviousness of scriptural knowledge, it is important to help people develop ways of making sense of it all. Perhaps if people have tools to help them understand the Bible, then they will read and study it more often. That is the hope of this book.

I.

What Is the Bible?

Hard to Read? Hard to Understand?

When I grew up, the King James translation of the Bible seemed to be the most widely used version; and while it's been replaced in popularity by other versions, it still has a large following. The problem I, like many others, had with that is that the King James uses language most people don't use today. It is an older form of the English language. We simply do not talk like that anymore, and that makes the Bible hard to read, understand, and explain. It was for this reason that when I began in ministry, I would take the passage of scripture–while "scripture" can refer to any sacred religious text, in this book I use "scripture" and "Bible" synonymously–I was preaching from and translate it to what I called *The Hip-Hop, New Jack Swing* translation. Basically, this meant interpreting the Bible for modern readers using language, phrases (slang), and images associated with hip-hop culture. This was a way to bring relevance to scripture that, for many, was hard to relate to. I soon discovered that there are other English translations besides the King James and the New King James versions. Most are more accurate and understandable than the King James. In fact, I had a Bible professor in seminary who did not allow students to use the King James translation. Regrettably, once you get beyond the language barrier those other translations are still hard to understand. The stories and images from millennia ago are so different from what we are accustomed to that it can turn people off.

As I have gone further in my ministerial career, I have had conversation after conversation with people who shared that they simply don't understand much of the Bible, regardless of what translation they use. In fact, one conversation I had was with a woman in her mid-forties who shared that she had been in the church her entire life and believed in God but a lot of the teachings of the Bible simply didn't make sense to her. There are countless people from various walks of life who share the same sentiment.

Even though many people don't understand or even believe a lot of the stories in scripture, the Bible remains a critical part of the Christian faith and Western culture in general. Perhaps that is the reason why so many Christians don't read it and rely solely on pastors to teach it, or what they know about the Bible comes from mere hearsay. Actually countless people subconsciously gain their understanding of scripture by way of Hollywood. I contend the idea that humans become angels after death comes directly from the gospel according to the movies.

How much of our belief comes from the gospel according to the movies?

Perhaps it is the Christmas classic *It's A Wonderful Life* that has led so many to expect the transition from human to angel once we pass from this physical life. I've heard people say at funerals that the deceased has gotten their wings. While it might be comforting to those who are grieving, it is not biblical. The truth of the matter is that the Bible does not teach that at all. To be perfectly real, the Bible essentially teaches that we will not only become greater than angels, but we will also judge them. Read 1 John 3:2, "Dear friends, now we are God's children, and it hasn't yet appeared what we will be. We know that when he appears we will be like him because we'll see him as he is." And 1 Corinthians 6:3 says, "Don't you know that we will judge angels? Why not ordinary things?" The him referred to in the first text is Jesus. That's right, we are going to be more like Jesus than angels. On top of all that, we, the followers of Jesus, will determine whether or not the actions of angels were right or wrong. My point is that what we think is found in the Bible often derives from a false premise from the very start.

All of this points to the reason why I felt it necessary to give some insights on what the Bible is, who it is for, and some approaches in reading the Bible that might help make sense of this very important yet confusing book. In addition to that, there are so many important and timeless lessons in the scriptures that can help and enhance countless more lives.

What Is the Word of God?

What did people do before there was a Bible? That is a very important question when it comes to faith and understanding God. Before there were any sacred writings for people to know about God or how to live for God, there was the Word of God. Now, I know when many people hear or read that phrase today, they immediately think about the Bible. To many "the Word of God" and "Bible" are synonymous. However, when we read that phrase in scripture, it is not referring to anything that is written down. The Word of God in the Bible is not a text; the phrase appears when people have received a message from God in some form or fashion outside of any written communication. In other words, these people believed God spoke to them and they understood that as the Word of God.

The Word of God, or the message from God, was sometimes given to men and women in the form of a dream or a sign. At other times it came from another person or an overwhelming sensation. In some instances, we don't know how exactly the Word came to someone except that we are told God spoke to them. In the case of Abram, whose name would be later changed to Abraham, Genesis 12:1-2 simply tells us that God spoke to him: "The LORD said to Abram, 'Leave your land, your family, and your father's household for the land that I will show you. I will make of you a great nation and will bless you. I will make your name respected, and you will be a blessing.'" How Abram received this message exactly we don't know, but Abram, and later his descendants, believed God spoke to him by some method and manner and gave him a message. And that is where all of this begins, with God revealing something to humanity–to people like you and me. Yes, like you and me.

The same is true when it comes to preaching. Anyone preaching a sermon believes they are declaring what God has spoken to them to share with others. Writing a sermon is an exercise of study and listening for God's voice. Yes, many (hopefully all) use the Bible as the primary basis of their preaching, but the interpretation, explanation, application, and the modernization of the stories still come from God's inspiration. Or at least we hope they do. Sermon preparation and preaching is a combination of understanding a passage of scripture and then prayerfully anticipating that God will speak to you and then through you for the benefit of others.

Let me see if I can make it more plain by explaining it like this. If the speaker does not hear from God, a sermon, at best, can only be inspirational and informative. However, when one hears from God, the sermon is more than inspirational and informative; it becomes transformative and life-enhancing. Hearing from God about a particular passage of scripture is why preachers preach in the first place. If it were simply a matter of reading the Bible then there would be no need for preachers to declare what God is saying for a particular time and context. The simple point is this: just like Abraham and others who did not have scripture to read, the modern preacher and believers in general can and do still receive the Word of God outside of the Bible. The Bible is a collection of what people believed God had said to them, and to their revered ancestors, sages, and leaders, as God's Word was passed down from generation to generation; the stories were carefully collected and written down by learned scribes and religious authorities at a much later time, but still over two thousand years ago.

The Word of God transforms and enhances our lives.

The first part of knowing God begins with God revealing God's truth to humanity. Next comes faith. That is to say, God can speak, but in order for people to truly hear it and then share it as God's Word, there must be faith. Without faith people might hear from God but not know it, accept it, or embrace it. They might interpret it as luck or coincidence. However, through the lens of faith, one can distinguish between those things and God's Word. I've often said that although some people declare that seeing is believing, I contend that there are some things you cannot hear or see unless you first believe.

When I received my calling from God to go into ministry it could have easily been misunderstood. I was with some friends about to go to a party. We were laughing and doing all the things young men in their twenties do before they go to a big party (wink wink). All of a sudden all of us hear someone say, "You know, one day I'm going to be a preacher." Then I noticed that everyone was looking at me. Somehow, without my thinking about it, those words came out of my mouth. I could have easily dismissed it as something that just happened. But through the lens of faith I was able to see that God was speaking to me.

We are born with a desire to know the truth of who we are.

While I don't claim we are born having faith (that can be debated), I do believe we have an innate desire within us to know the truth of our existence. I believe it is that innate desire that leads us to seek out truth and puts us in a position to encounter God and come to have faith. I believe that's why Abram could hear from God and that's why we today have the ability and opportunity to hear from God. In short, the Bible is a collection of what God has spoken to others. So, it all begins with God speaking and people of faith hearing, explaining, and sharing. The New Testament was written decades after the life, death, and resurrection of Jesus. The way the story survived was through witnesses to the resurrection sharing it with family, friends, and as many people as they could in the Middle East, Africa, Asia, and Europe. That oral tradition was eventually written down as were letters to various faith communities. Today we call this group of writings the New Testament.

The Word of God can be understood as God speaking to humanity, and the Gospel of John in the New Testament explains how Jesus is the Word of God. In the first three verses of chapter one of John we learn that everything God created comes from God's Word: "In the beginning was the Word and the Word was with God and the Word was God. The Word was with God in the beginning. Everything came into being through the Word, and without the Word nothing came into being." John is sharing that everything that is became reality when God spoke it into existence. Then when you jump down to verse 14, it says, "The Word became flesh and made his home among us. We have seen his glory, glory like that of a father's only son, full of grace and truth." That's right, God's Word became a living organism and was completely embodied in the person of Jesus of Nazareth. And that living, breathing Word in the person of Jesus healed, taught, walked on water, died for our sins, and was raised from the dead. His story was told, retold, and eventually shared in written form in what we call the Gospels of Matthew, Mark, Luke, and John. So in one sense it is understandable that people refer to the Bible as the Word of God.

Who Wrote the Bible?

I once heard a nonbeliever say, "God doesn't write books." The first thought I had was, "How do you know?" The thought behind the statement from the agnostic is that the Bible was written not by God but by humans. Furthermore, it implies that if God had something to say, God wouldn't put it down on paper. Why wouldn't God just say it directly to whomever the message was for? I would agree, but what if when God spoke to that person, he or she wanted to write it down so that others would come to know what the writer had experienced or witnessed? I would also say if you are not sure God exists in the first place, can you really speak about what God does or does not do?

While we will talk more about who wrote the Bible and how it came to be later in this book, I do want to say I believe it is helpful for people to write down what they believe God says to them. Just as with science, medicine, or psychology, we learn from previous generations. We build upon the knowledge of those who came before us. If we did not have their written or oral accounts of their discoveries and conclusions, we would not be able to advance as a society, and we would not have much of the progress we enjoy today. It is the same with our understanding of God. Without a written account of who God is and how God operates from generations past, we could not progress as a species or, more specifically, grow as people of faith.

Having said all of that it is important to note there is another critical reason why people chose to write down the stories in what we call the Bible, and that is revelation. God has and continues to reveal certain things to individuals and communities of faith. If people believe that God has spoken to them, wouldn't it make sense to share it either in oral or written form? Here is the reason why. Human beings can acquire knowledge through experience, experimentation, and exploration, but it all happens within some kind of community. You can't attain true knowledge in isolation or else it would not be understandable to you, let alone anyone else. Even the words we say and the images we dream have roots in a community. And because we are finite, limited creatures we can only come to know so much about the infinite, especially when it comes to the creation of the universe and metaphysics, that is to say, the structure, function, meaning, purpose, and nature of things.

We as limited creatures can only obtain so much knowledge and understanding on our own. And there is a lot that we are able to figure out. But there is still so much we don't know. Sometimes it takes a lifetime even to know who we are or who our friends are. Think about it like this: scientists only understand about five percent of the brain and we have only explored 5 percent of the ocean. That being the case, can you really say that you comprehend the deep truths of the universe on your own?

True, God did create us with brains so we can attain some knowledge on our own. We can even come to know about God or the universal order on our own. But even that is because we are created so that we can recognize order and create our versions of order or chaos. However, our human nature has limits, and beyond those limits God must reveal the rest. So one could argue that one way God reveals what human beings can gain on their own is for it to be written down by people that it's been revealed to. Why would we then ignore it or put it aside as irrelevant? Are we arrogant enough to believe that we know more today about just about everything? Keep in mind we do know more when it comes to medicine, technology, and science, because we were able to build upon what those who came before us learned and recorded ages ago.

What Is the Bible?

Most people are familiar with the Bible but are probably unaware of what it truly is. I'm going to explain this in very straightforward terms. On the cover of most Bibles you have the word "holy." Many people refer to it not simply as the Bible but as the Holy Bible. So, what is the Holy Bible? The word "holy" refers to principled and ethical completeness or faultlessness. It means complete autonomy with no impurity or evil. "Sanctified" and "holy" are synonymous in that they both denote being set apart from sin, set apart for righteousness or right living.

Sin is what separates us from God, because to sin is to miss the mark established by God. God, to be sure, is the only one who is holy, the only one who is perfect and without sin and completely righteous. However, God requires holy living from all. So when you read the cover of the scriptures and see the word "holy," please know it is referring to perfection and sinlessness. In essence what the word "holy" on the cover of a book of scripture denotes is a way of life, a way in which we have to depend on God, because we are not and cannot be holy.

God wants us to be in a right relationship with God and with each other.

After the word "holy" is the word "Bible." What does that mean? Where does the word "Bible" come from? The word "Bible" originates from the French and Latin translations of the Greek word that means "books."[1] So what we have is a book made up of different books that sets out a standard of living and a way to meet that standard. We can think of the Bible as a library of books written at different times for different purposes, but together they record God's Word as it has variously been understood over a long period of time.

It is also worth mentioning that in the fourth century the word "canon," which means "measuring rod," came into play. This is because representatives of the entire Church decided which books would become scripture and in what order they would be placed in the Bible. They, in essence, took measure of all the possible writings and selected the ones they believed were most accurate, most trusted, and written by those who were witnesses, or close associates of witnesses, of Jesus's life, death, and resurrection. That is why it is not uncommon to use the word "canon" when referring to the Bible. This sense of the word "canon" had already been put to use by a second-century African Christian scholar by the name of Origen. In seminary my professors commonly referred to the Bible as the Canon. When I first heard it, I was afraid we were going to have to learn about the Bible and then study something called the Canon. As the Holy Bible is truly a canon, then what we have is a book of perfection and sinlessness that is a measuring rod for our lives. In other words, it is what believers use as a standard for measuring their lives, spiritual and otherwise.

Now, you may have read this holy measuring rod and said there are plenty of people in the Bible who were just the opposite of holy. There were people full of sin and far from perfect. In that way the people of the Bible are like us. In fact, there are leading figures in the Bible who had major flaws. There was Noah who liked to drink, get drunk, get naked, and then get mad that his son Ham saw him naked. That doesn't sound very holy to me. Then of course there are Adam and Eve, who disobeyed God and ate from the very tree that God told them not to eat from. Jonah tried to run from God's call on his life. He didn't want to preach to save the Ninevites from destruction, because they were not a part of his social circle.

Even Moses, the man who led the Israelites out of Egyptian bondage, had some flaws. He killed an Egyptian and tried to hide the body in the sand. Moses even disobeyed God by not following through on instructions God gave him. When the Israelites were in the wilderness in need of water, God responded to their pleas. God told Moses to speak to a rock, and Moses struck the rock but did not speak to it, which resulted in him not being able to enter into the new land of promise. Why he was supposed to speak to an inanimate object does not matter; the point is that Moses disobeyed God.

I'm sure you are thinking, "How is it that this book we call the Bible can be called holy? Moreover, why should I use it or look to people to be a measuring rod for my life?" Whether or not a life is holy depends on how the life story is told. That is to say, one's life is holy or unholy based on how you tell your story, and please know that everyone has a story. If you look at how those stories are told in the Bible and how we tell history, there is a big difference. While some people want to read the Bible like a historical document, they need to understand that it is not. I don't believe it was ever intended to be a history book as we understand it. We know history books teach the who, what, when, and where and are generally light on the how and why. On the other hand, the Bible is heavy on the why and how and light on the when, where, and what unless it is relevant to the why and how.

Whether or not a life is holy depends on how the life story is told.

Let me give you an example of the difference. History's version of the Montgomery Bus Boycott of 1955 is that African Americans in Montgomery refused to ride city buses until they were treated fairly. The rule of law was that African Americans had to sit in the back of the bus. And if the bus was full, they had to give up their seats to white passengers. The black citizens of Montgomery wanted the right to sit wherever they wanted on the bus. After all, if someone pays for something, they ought to be able to receive the same services as the next person who pays. The boycott was sparked by Rosa Parks refusing to give up her seat for a white man (which was the custom) and move to the back of the bus. For a year African Americans walked and carpooled faithfully, and it began to hurt the bus company financially. Finally, after lots of negotiations the bus company gave in and allowed all people of every race to sit wherever they wanted. That's history, or at least the most commonly accepted version.

If the biblical writers told the story it might go something like this. After prayer and contemplation African Americans relied on God to get them where they needed to be. They put their complete trust in God to protect them and transport them from place to place for an entire year. Through persistence and trust in God, things changed drastically. God changed the minds of the bus company executives, and African Americans were victorious.

Do you see the difference? One version explains what happened in a tangible and reasonable way. The other version isn't as concerned about the minute details of the story. What's important in this retelling is who is responsible for making it happen, and the responsible party is God. The people involved were instruments of God's will. Both stories are true but only one of the stories could be considered holy.

Let me give another example, a biblical example. Take the story of the ten plagues of Egypt found in the Exodus story. This is where God told Moses to demand that the king of Egypt release the Hebrew slaves. The king, called Pharaoh, refused to let the people go, thus unleashing God to do something about it in the form of ten plagues. These were the ten plagues: the Nile River turned to blood, the land was saturated with frogs, then lice, then insect swarms, then pestilence, then boils, then hail, then locusts, then darkness, and finally the death of every firstborn son and animal in Egypt. I've actually watched a few documentaries where they sought to explain these things scientifically. The Nile River turning to what biblical writers termed "blood" was perhaps caused by a red algae bloom, which would have made the water appear as blood. Each plague that followed resulted in a domino effect of the red algae bloom.

That makes perfect sense to me. I can accept that as what actually happened. It is the scientific explanation of an unusual event. However, none of that really mattered to the biblical writers, even if they knew that was the honest-to-God truth. The only important point of the story is that God made it happen. How it happened is irrelevant. God caused all of that to happen for the purpose of leading the Pharaoh of Egypt to the conclusion that he must release God's people, the Israelites.

Not only do people make the mistake of reading the Bible as a history book, but they also look at it sometimes as a sociology book or science book. They want explanations of certain things that biblical writers were not necessarily concerned about. For example, one of the first questions people have about the Bible is "Where did all the people come from?" God created Adam and Eve and they had sons and those sons got married. What? Where did the women come from? Now, there are various traditions outside of the Bible that explain how Cain and Abel were able to marry women. However, the Bible does not mention other people being created. So where did they come from? And how do we get all the various races we have today? If you asked the biblical writers that question they would probably look at you strangely and might even ask why it matters. Because the point of the story is not really about the people but about God. The most important thing in the story is that God created everything in existence. The biblical writers were not concerned about the explanation of race (they did not live in a racially structured society as we do today) or the development of various peoples. To ponder those things is fine but that's not the purpose of the book of Genesis. It was not written to explain everything, it was designed to share what God has done and is doing in creation.

I always say, if you want to read about history don't read the Bible, and if you want to know about science then go read science books. But if you want to know about people and God's relationship to people, then read the Bible. And remember those history and science books might actually help you understand the Bible better.

History and science books might help you better understand the Bible. But the Bible will teach you about people.

You see, the Bible is far from a historical or scientific document. It is the story of God's interaction in the world through a particular people. What makes this book a holy measuring rod is that there is a lot of God language in it. It's God's story told through the lens of human experience. Because God is the only one who is perfect, then the only way you and I can become perfect is by having God as part of our stories. The Bible is called holy not because the people were sinless, but because they included God in their stories. In all actuality they inserted themselves in God's story.

The biblical story begins in Genesis chapter one verse one with "In the beginning God created . . ." so it starts with God and God is involved in the heart of the story (Genesis 1:1, NIV). The story ends in Revelation with the words, "The grace of the Lord Jesus be with God's people. Amen" (Revelation 22:21, NIV). So the story ends and begins with God. One's life story only becomes holy when God is included. No matter how many nice things you say to people, your life is not holy unless God is at the beginning of your story, in the middle of your story, and at the end of your story. What makes a story holy is who gets the credit for the good and positive things. In the book that we call the Holy Bible, everything that happened was credited to God—not partially credited to God; the Almighty got all the recognition. We too give God credit, but far too often we only give God credit for certain things. But what we learn from the Bible is that all good things come from God. Therefore, the way you measure your life to the standard set by this book is by examining how God fits into your story.

As you read on in the Bible you discover in the New Testament that God gave the world a living measuring rod to follow. Jesus came as a model of perfection and sinlessness. In fact, God is so good that God gave God's son to be perfect on our behalf, and all you have to do is include Jesus in your life story. When you do, you become part of Jesus's holy story. What that means is that everything Jesus inherits from God, we also inherit. In short, the Bible is the story of God, who helps us measure up by showing us how to live and then helping us do it. If you allow Jesus to do that, you are making God part of your personal story.

How Did We Get the Bible?

The Bible is a collection of books written by many authors who tell the story of God's interaction with and action in the world through the descendants, and later adopted heirs, of Abraham. Abraham was a man born in Ur of the Chaldeans (modern-day Iraq). He and his wife, Sarah, were the patriarch and matriarch of those who became known as God's people (Genesis 11:26-17:27). The scriptures were not intended to explain everything about the world but were meant to be a guide, helping us learn from what happened in the past, that is, how God was faithful. As I stated earlier, the Bible is not a history book, nor is it a science book. It is a sacred book that reveals to us more than we could ever learn about God on our own.

The Bible could be broken down into categories. The Old Testament is made up of the law in the first five books (Genesis through Deuteronomy). The next twelve books (Joshua through Esther) make up the history portion. Then, the next five books (Job through the Song of Solomon) make up the wisdom or poetry literature. The next five books (Isaiah, Jeremiah, Lamentations, Ezekiel, and Daniel) make up what's known as the major prophets–called major because of their length. The next twelve books are the minor prophets (minor because they are shorter than the major prophets). These books start with Hosea and end with Malachi.

The first four books of the New Testament–Matthew, Mark, Luke, and John–make up the Gospels. The book of Acts gives an account of how the Church came into being. Next comes a group of epistles or letters written, or so it is thought, by the Apostle Paul. These are Romans through Philemon. What are called the general epistles (written by various people) include Hebrews through Jude. These letters originate from the apostles and their followers. The epistles attributed to the Apostle Paul are each addressed to a specific community of faith or an individual person. The general epistles are named after the authors and seem to have been written to the faith community more broadly. The last book, Revelation, is considered a book of prophecy. Like the book of Daniel in the Old Testament, it is known as apocalyptic literature. This means that these books unveil or reveal things not previously known.

Many people believe that there is value in all parts of the Bible, but many other questions remain. Some question whether or not the Bible is still applicable or if it ever was. If all scripture comes from God, then the immediate question becomes "How?" How did the scripture come from God and to whom? The next question is, "How should we use the Bible so that it can help and educate its readers?" Others ask: "Do you have to belong to or believe in God for the scripture to be useful?" And, "Who in reality belongs to God?"

Every scripture is inspired by God and is useful for teaching, for showing mistakes, for correcting, and for training character, so that the person who belongs to God can be equipped to do everything that is good. (2 Timothy 3:16-17)

There are those who believe God spoke every word to the authors of the Bible and the writers wrote it down word for word. The reality is that's not exactly how it happened. Most of the books of the Bible were written generations after the actual events. There is no one author for these books. They came from priests, scribes, prophets, kings, apostles, and the disciples of those leaders. The purpose of writing things down was to share lessons that had been learned from the successes and failures of previous generations. The purpose was to ensure that God's people worshipped only God and that they lived like God's people in a right relationship with God, each other, and foreigners.

When the Israelites were defeated in war or taken into captivity, they believed it was a result of disobeying God. In the same manner, whenever they won a battle or experienced any kind of prosperity, it was a result of obedience to God. So when the writers of the various books shared the positive and negative experiences of Israel, it was to show future generations the importance of obeying God and the dangers of disobedience. That's how the Bible serves as a book of correction and training. We read of other people's triumphs and failures and the consequences and rewards associated with them and act accordingly. It was really to help later people develop a relationship with God. In that sense, the motivation for writing the scriptures came from God and was inspired by God.

The writers of the Bible also struggled with why bad things happen to good people. They were aware, as are we, that sometimes a person can live right, believe right, do right by others, and still suffer tragedy and hardship. The book of Job and many psalms address this. But the answer the biblical writers give is to trust God no matter what, and that is relevant still today.

Who the scriptures were written for is the same as who wrote them in the first place. The scriptures were written by and for the descendants of Abraham, Isaac (Abraham's son), and Jacob (Isaac's son). Each had other children, but the record of God's Word, including God's promises, as the Bible describes it, was handed down this way. However, when you get to the New Testament, God's Word becomes available even to those who aren't direct descendants of Abraham.

The New Testament was written for those who were followers of Jesus of Nazareth—which was a village in Galilee—who was a Jew, a descendant of Abraham, Isaac, and Jacob, as were his first followers. But the inspiration and motivation for writing the New Testament was a desire to enable other people, beyond the family of Abraham, to know and be in relationship with God and to understand what God had done for the entire world through Jesus.

The followers of Jesus also believed and still believe that it was under the influence of the Holy Spirit that the 27 books of the New Testament were written. In all actuality I think it's safe to say that many modern followers of Jesus also believe that the Old Testament was written under the influence of God's Holy Spirit. The bottom line for the Old and New Testaments is that people who believed in the one and only God wrote down stories, lessons, and instructions based on what they had learned about God for the sake of helping others gain an understanding and appreciation for God so that they could live fruitful lives.

It's important to remember, as my New Testament professor used to say, that the Bible wasn't written for you, at least not directly. That is to say, the authors did not have you and your modern cultural understanding in mind when they wrote the scriptures. They were writing to a specific context, but that does not mean that what was meant for people long ago can't still apply to us today. God spoke to ancient people through the scripture, and God speaks to us through that same scripture. Each generation has had a different way of viewing the world, but each book was written with a specific people in mind, and those people had a specific worldview that is very different from ours. But when it comes down to it, people are people no matter when they lived. We love. They loved. We make mistakes. They did too. We want what we want when we want it. They were no different.

In order to get the intent of scripture, we must place ourselves, as best we can, into the minds of the original recipients. We can miss the true point or the spirit of a text by forgetting that the author and recipients did not think like we do. While it may not have been written with twenty-first-century readers in mind, the Bible was always intended to be passed down from one generation to the next and address the unique needs of each generation.

The biblical authors wrote about God's interaction in the world with the assumption that the readers or hearers had knowledge of the backdrop of the story. When the Bible was written the average person could not read and fewer had access to any books, even scriptures. Therefore, most people would have only heard scripture read in worship or educational settings. James M. Hamilton Jr., in his book *What Is Biblical Theology?*, calls this the "interpretive perspective."[2] That is to say, the authors of the Bible wrote from the perspective of their understanding of earlier sacred texts as well as liberating historical events that were important to them and their readers/hearers.

While the original messages throughout the Bible were not intended for us from the authors' perspectives, God knew later people would read the Bible and, I believe, intended for people of every succeeding generation to read it and use it as a guide. Therefore, no true modern attempt to interpret scripture should or can accurately be done without the belief that God has a lesson to teach us. Furthermore, we can trust and hope that God's Spirit will reveal the contextual meaning for particular texts to those who truly want to know the truths within the pages of the Bible.

Please don't take the previous statement to mean that the process of interpretation falls solely on God. We have a role to play. Our job is to examine, question, and seek the truth, and God will do the rest. Often that's how God operates, working in partnership with us–though not necessarily a 50-50 partnership. We take one step and God carries us several steps. We do the light lifting and God does the heavy lifting.

When we read the Bible with the understanding that it was designed with the purpose of providing instruction and guidance, we realize that we are free to put it into practice in our daily living. When we read the Bible as a history book or as something other than what it is, we can get lost or bogged down. If we can learn to read the Bible in a manner that instructs, corrects, and builds up our character, we'll be on the right path. I will talk in later chapters about how that can happen.

The Bible is also not a rule book. It is not something we should open randomly and rely on the first thing we read to determine what we should or should not do. The Bible is made up of stories within a larger story, God's story. One should not look at the Bible the same as we would bylaws of an organization. That's a dangerous thing to do. It would be like taking the rules of an organization that you don't belong to and applying it to a different organization altogether. The laws in the Bible, specifically the Old Testament, were written within a certain context that may not connect with what we know and do today. It's like taking a round peg and trying to put it in a rectangular hole. Therefore, one should not read the Bible as if it is merely a book of laws that we jump in and adhere to but should rather glean moral lessons from the story. Sure, there are expectations in scripture, such as the Ten Commandments, and there are things we should be very mindful of. After all, the Ten Commandments are not suggestions but universal laws that are applicable to every generation, but even they must be read in context. But more importantly, we are to learn from the mistakes and triumphs of people who had a deep relationship and connection with the same God that we do.

How Do We Read the Bible in Context?

The reason why different people understand the Bible differently is because we all have our own experiences and contexts. It is impossible to read the Bible and understand it from the perspective of someone whose culture, language, and tradition are completely different from yours. Even when we read the Bible at different stages of our lives, it speaks to us differently. So whose interpretation and understanding is correct?

Fortunately, or some might say unfortunately, there is more than one way of approaching and understanding the holy scriptures. It's like having several people standing around a large building. Everyone is looking at the same building, but they are standing on different sides. If you ask them to report on what they see, you will get several different answers, and all of them could be correct. It's the same building but from different vantage points. People stand on different sides of the Bible because we have different contexts. But what's important is that we are looking at the same book.

We see the Bible differently because we each have our own context.

That's not to say that everyone can simply come up with their own interpretation. Not all opinions have the same value. Some people spend their entire lives studying the Bible, its original languages, its history. These are people of faith. They seek to know the whole story and not just this or that part. It doesn't mean that there are no standards by which the Bible should be interpreted. There have to be some principles and concepts on which we can agree, and I will talk about those later. Those universally accepted principles and truths help us relate the scripture to our personal, and often changing, perspective.

To be sure, when trying to understand the Bible, it is helpful to name your reality. For example, I read the Bible from the perspective of an African American male who grew up listening to hip-hop music, worshipping in a predominately African American United Methodist church, and attending a predominately white Catholic School. I can go on, but I think you get the point. I cannot separate the truths about myself and all the experiences that come along with them as I seek to find meaning and purpose in scripture.

The reality is the various books of the Bible were written by, presumably, Jewish men. They wrote from a male's point of view, because they were unable, just as I am, to write from a woman's point of view. So the reason we read that God is a male is because that's how men identify with God. It is very likely that if women wrote the scriptures in a matriarchal society, we would see more feminine language about God than we do masculine. But I know, as I hope you do as well, that God cannot be just male because scripture says that females were created in God's image. God is bigger than one gender because God is infinitely more than we can imagine.

The mistake we make is thinking that we read the Bible from a completely unfiltered perspective. That's simply not true. Everything we take in is filtered through our own personal cultural lens. In the same sense it is helpful when trying to understand scripture to identify your personal cultural lens. It might explain why some passages are troubling to you and why others are meaningful. Those same passages that you might find troubling might be meaningful to someone else and the ones you find delightful might be hurtful to others.

Two quick examples of this: one is the language about being a slave for Christ that the Apostle Paul uses in Romans 1:1, "From Paul, a slave of Christ Jesus, called to be an apostle and set apart for God's good news." Some people are untroubled and easily get the point that Paul is trying to make, but for others it is a very disturbing image. They don't want to think of themselves in the terms of being a slave. There is a long, brutal history tied to the word "slavery" in many parts of the world, but in particular the Americas.

Another word that might cause some pain, and there are many others, is the word "father" being applied to God. To many that is a fantastic image because of the relationship they have with their fathers. For others that image causes pain because of the relationship or the lack thereof they had with their fathers. Still others might even ask the question, "Well, can I think of God as mother rather than father?" That is an excellent question and the simple answer is yes. While it is not often lifted up, there are a few passages of scripture that make reference to God as mother, most notably Isaiah 66:13, "As a mother comforts her child, so I will comfort you; in Jerusalem you will be comforted." Understanding and accepting your personal context is critical when trying to find meaning in scripture.

Do you have to belong to God in order for the Bible to be for you? The easy answer is no. While it may have been originally intended for people who already have a relationship with God, it can be just as helpful for those who don't. I would argue that the Bible is equally for people who don't believe in God, because part of what is taught in scripture, especially the New Testament, is to share the good news with those who don't know the good news. To be honest, if the scripture is for all who belong to God, then in essence it is for everyone. "The earth is the LORD's and everything in it, the world and its inhabitants too" (Psalm 24:1). That being the case, scripture was written for you, regardless of where you are in your relationship or lack thereof with God. Most would consider those who belong to God to be those who believe and acknowledge that they belong to God. But to be clear, God created everyone, so everyone, in essence, belongs to God. It's just that some embrace faith in God, others are unaware of it, and some ignore it. Yet all are precious in the sight of God. God is God no matter who you are or what you believe about God.

II.

Why Is the Bible Important?

What Is the Value of Scripture?

The Bible is the number-one-selling book of all time and there is a good reason for it. People buy it (whether they read it or not is another question altogether) because they see value in it. I believe that everyone has an innate yearning in them, whether they truly recognize it or not, to know and unite with the Creator. After all, God created us all; therefore, we have within us the longing to reconnect with our Maker. That's one of the reasons why so many people buy and keep Bibles in their homes. While many people may not read it, understand it, or even believe it all, they are aware of the claims that the Bible holds universal truths about life. It is out of that awareness that many people have some sort of respect for the Bible.

The Bible teaches that it is God's intent for humanity to have a strong and right relationship with God. Ever since the first disobedience of humanity with Adam and Eve, God has been working to bring people back into a good and perfect relationship with God and with each other. Restoring that relationship and keeping us connected with God was the purpose of events in the story of Noah and the flood. It is also the reason God established commandments. And when those commandments were not kept, God sent prophet after prophet, all for the purpose of reestablishing the relationship with humanity that was broken as a result of humanity's inevitable inclination to stray, rebel, and disobey God. Even with our best intentions, we cannot help being selfish and tripping ourselves up with self-defeating behavior. This is what is known as the Fall of Humanity. Yet, limited and mistake-prone as we are, God wants to be in relationship with us.

The Bible Tells God's Story

What makes the Bible so valuable is that it tells the story of God. Through the stories of Israel (the descendants of Jacob, the grandson of Abraham), we learn who God is and what God requires. We even learn what it means to have a relationship with God–what it looks like. In the book of Genesis, the story shows Abram, whose name was later changed to Abraham, talking with God as though they are friends. There's even a story where Abraham bargains with God and tries to talk God out of destroying two cities just as casually as you might try to talk a friend out of wearing a certain outfit (Genesis 18). That shows us that we can develop a relationship with the Creator of the universe, a deep, close personal relationship where we can talk to God like a friend. Would we know that without the story in scripture?

By reading the books of Jeremiah and Lamentations you see another example of someone who had such a good relationship with God that he could be completely honest with God. In fact, Jeremiah was so open with God that he actually blamed God for the suffering he was experiencing. His family and friends mocked and ridiculed him because of the ministry that God had called him to. And Jeremiah let God know his displeasure with the suffering that came along with his calling into prophetic ministry. At the same time

Jeremiah also expressed his trust in God to see him through his troubles. Again it is through scripture we find this kind of relationship with the Creator of all things, and it shows that we too can have that type of relationship. The Bible shows us that we can be completely honest with God whether we think God is good, bad, or indifferent. By knowing God, we learn that God is only good. God is the definition of goodness, love, power, and mercy. God is not evil and God is definitely not indifferent, but how would you know if you didn't have the Bible to show you?

The Bible Tells Us What God Requires

It is from the scriptures that we learn what God requires of us. In Exodus chapter 20 God gives Moses the Ten Commandments. These commandments, not suggestions, were given as a guide to the people, so they would know how to live in community together. The Ten Commandments were meant to set the tone for how people treated one another and how they were to relate to God. How else would we know how to connect with others and God if we did not have the Bible to give us the example? This is why scripture is so valuable.

There is also story after story about how God responds when we disobey what God requires. We see punishment upon God's people (the Israelites) because of idolatry and mistreatment of the poor. Those two themes we will talk about later. Sometimes their penalty was bondage and the ruin of their society. Please keep in mind that's the way the biblical writers thought about things during that period. They believed that if they did wrong there was punishment from God and if they did right God would reward them. However, today we might simply call that cause and effect. That is to say, every action has a reaction. Even though we learn from scripture how God responds to disobedience, it is more important to see that God always forgives people. This suggests to us, as we read and try to understand the Bible, that God is a forgiving God.

The Bible Shows Us That God Is Loving

Another reason why the Bible is important is because it teaches us just how loving God really is. It was out of love that God entered human history as a human being–Jesus of Nazareth. Jesus was born and raised in poverty in a backwater province of the Roman Empire after leaving the riches of the universe. Think about that: to willingly give up the best that the universe has to offer in order to make a sacrifice for others. Jesus endured ridicule, betrayal, abandonment, and denial from close friends. He was falsely arrested and sentenced to death, which might be one of the many reasons why black and brown people can relate with Jesus so well. Jesus was then tortured, humiliated by being made to carry a heavy wooden cross through the streets of Jerusalem, and then nailed to it. Although he could have easily put all of this to an end he did not. He could have returned to his rightful place next to the Father at the throne of grace. However, he chose to stay and endure to the end simply because he loved us too much.

God forgives and God loves us.

Jesus's earthly experiences showed humanity just how much God loves us. They also show that God can relate to us, because as a human, God experienced the same things we experience: joy, hunger, sadness–everything. He knows what it means to be hungry, cold, tired, disappointed, in pain, and all the other negative things that go along with being mortal.

The Bible Relays God's Plan

The Bible is also important because it relays God's plan for the salvation of the world. There is no way humanity could possibly figure out on our own what our eternal fate would or could be. Such knowledge comes only because God revealed it to someone who shared it with us, the future generations, through the pages of scripture. We know Jesus's coming into the world served the purpose of rescuing humanity from its sinful self. Jesus died on the cross as the ultimate sacrifice offered up to God for the world. Again, this is something that can only be known if it is revealed to us.

The Bible Tells Us God's Endgame

Not only does the Bible share God's plan for salvation but it also describes for us, because of God's revelation to biblical writers, what God's kingdom is like, what God's endgame is for us. There are several parables in the Gospels–Matthew, Mark, Luke, and John–that talk about this. In them Jesus explains how one gains access to the kingdom and how to be great in the kingdom of God. Jesus, having firsthand knowledge of what the kingdom of God is like, could only explain it to us using human images and symbols. God's kingdom is beyond human imagination and we can't comprehend it in full, at least not in this life. However, we get a glimpse of it through the parables of Jesus.

The Bible Tells Us God's Strategy

The Bible is important because it conveys God's plan to bring every human being back into right relationship with God. That is to say, God's strategy is to spread the good news about God's liberating and steadfast loving-kindness as personified by Jesus to the world so people can accept and embrace it. The strategy is simple yet seemingly risky. To quote Loki from the Marvel movie *Avengers*, we the followers of Jesus are "burdened with glorious purpose." We have been given the task of taking part in the building of God's kingdom on earth so that it reflects heaven.

There is a story that after Jesus was raised from the grave and ascended into heaven, he had a conversation with the angels. They asked him about his time on earth. Jesus shared with them that he met a few people who followed him and listened to his teachings. "However, when I was in my most desperate hour, they abandoned me." Jesus went on to share with the angels how he was crucified and how crowds chose a criminal over him. "But, after the resurrection I reconnected with my friends who had abandoned me," Jesus explained. The angels asked Jesus what his plan was to spread the news of salvation to the world. Jesus responded by informing them that he left the task to his followers and they would share it with others and so on. The angels were perplexed because they knew that when trusting in a bunch of human beings, things could easily go wrong. So the angels asked Jesus a very reasonable question, "What's your backup plan?" Jesus responded, "I don't have a backup plan. I'm trusting that those who love me will continue to share the news with others and work to create heaven on earth." While the story is fictitious, the moral of the story is true. The plan to make the world a better place is up to all of the followers of Jesus.

The Bible Shows Us What God Is Like

In addition to all of those things, as we read about the life, teachings, and legacy of Jesus we get a glimpse into God's personality–what God is like. Have you ever wondered what God is like? Mark 1:40-42 tells the story of how Jesus showed sympathy and healed a man with leprosy. It says, "A man with a skin disease approached Jesus, fell to his knees, and begged, 'If you want, you can make me clean.' Incensed, Jesus reached out his hand, touched him, and said, 'I do want to. Be clean.' Instantly, the skin disease left him, and he was clean."

That story shows, through the actions of Jesus, that God is compassionate and sympathetic to the pain and suffering of others. We see God's love and compassion again when Jesus is dying on a cross. Through what must have been unimaginable pain, he looks down at the people ridiculing him and forgives them. In Luke 23:34, in the midst of pain and agony, "Jesus said, 'Father, forgive them, for they don't know what they're doing.' They drew lots [gambled] as a way of dividing up his clothing." That reveals God's nature of forgiveness–even when we stray far from God, even when we try to extinguish God's influence from our lives. There are many other stories where Jesus shows kindness, generosity, and patience that help us better understand who God is.

Jesus shows us that God does not condone unfair cultural practices. Jesus defied custom and tradition by including women in his teaching and healing ministry. The custom of Jesus's day was that men did not discuss issues of God with women in public, yet Jesus broke that tradition. In John chapter 4 Jesus has a conversation with a Samaritan woman. This in and of itself was unusual because Jews and Samaritans were bitter rivals. Yet Jesus breaks the intolerance barrier that separates these groups and connects with someone from a different background, a different race, a different religion. Furthermore, Jesus also disrupts the practices of the day by engaging in a meaningful dialogue with a woman.

Jesus and this unnamed woman talk about God in a public setting. This broke all the social norms of society in that day. The conversation goes so well that in the end Jesus reveals that he is the messiah. Their conversation concludes this way in John 4:25-26, "The woman said, 'I know that the Messiah is coming, the one who is called the Christ. When he comes, he will teach everything to us.' Jesus said to her, 'I Am—the one who speaks with you.'"

We are "burdened with glorious purpose."

Jesus shows that there is a difference between the cultural way of doing things and God's way of doing things. Then he gives this woman a job, to tell her village about who he is. By the way, if you didn't know, God's way is always right. That's what the Bible teaches us and that's why the Bible matters.

Who Is the Bible For?

Once you move beyond the original intended readers, you can come to the conclusion that the Bible is actually for every person of every era. Because if it's God's story and God is the creator of all, then the book must be for everyone. But it is also tailor-made for you. Think about it like this. The writers of the Bible were flawed individuals and they wrote about flawed individuals who, in spite of their shortcomings, were loved by God. So if you have any flaws, you are in the same company as those we read about in the Bible and the ones for whom it was written in the first place. And you are equally loved by God.

To be sure, the Bible is a perfect tool for those who are searching for meaning and purpose in life. Those who are curious about eternal truths and really want to know why we exist in the first place–the Bible is for them. The Bible is for people who sense that there is more to life than meets the eye. While the Bible doesn't give direct answers to all of your questions, it provides stories and wisdom that can open your eyes and imagination to help you come to those conclusions. Perhaps the reason why many of the mysteries of life are not answered directly, but rather indirectly, is so that people will explore on their own.

A widely used passage of scripture is found in Matthew 7:7, where Jesus explains to his followers this very notion, "Ask, and you will receive. Search, and you will find. Knock, and the door will be opened to you." That is to say, the answers are there, but it requires that you search for them. Now, I'm sure some will say, "Why didn't God just make it plain and simple?" We wouldn't have to search if the biblical writers just came out and gave the answers to life's toughest questions. However, when you search, that requires time and effort, and that means you are invested in it. You tend to have more connection and attachment to something if you have to work for it. On the other hand, if you don't have to put time and effort into something, you tend not to have as much of an attachment to it. It's easy to take for granted those things that are simple.

God loves us all as if each of us is the only one.

I have a friend who is a counselor. She says that people come to her with all kinds of questions. But over the years she has learned not to give, or often even suggest, solutions. If she does, invariably the person reacts to her. But if she helps someone come to their own conclusions, even if they were obvious to her, the person has a much better chance of acting on them.

I believe the reason we must search for answers is because it is God's way of saying, "I want you to spend time with me by reading and studying scripture." If the answers came too easily then we might not even pick up the Bible. We wouldn't need to because we'd have all the answers we need. However, if you have to search, then you must spend more and more time reading, that is, spending time with God. When we spend more time with God, not only do we find meaning and purpose in life, but we find peace and joy. It's like watching one of those movies that has a very complicated plot. The first time you watch it you may understand the movie; when you watch it again, however, you understand some things you didn't notice at first. And every time you watch the movie, it seems as if you pick up something new. It is sort of like the 2000 movie *Memento,* where the main character, who has short-term memory loss, is trying to find his wife's murderer. However, it is extremely difficult because he can't remember anything. The movie requires that you give it your full attention, because many things are not as simple as they seem. If you turn away for a second, it is easy to miss an important clue. That's how reading the Bible can be. The more you read it, the more you understand and know. In short, the Bible is for anyone and everyone who wants more out of life than the superficial.

Looking for Proof?

The fact that people want proof is nothing new, and it certainly is not something related to the Bible alone. One of the questions that some of us may wrestle with is how we know if the Bible is really inspired by God. Is there any proof that would back up the claim that, while God did not write the Bible, it nevertheless does come from God? The truth of the matter is that it is not something that anyone can prove. At the same time no one can disprove it either. Where does that leave us? It's easy to say that it's a matter of faith and we just have to believe it. For many modern readers, especially the younger generations, that answer is not good enough. So for those who need some sort of evidence, I can offer this: The Bible has stood the test of time. Consider that we have a collection of books that have been passed down for two millennia–and the Old Testament writings are even older. Working from the principles of this collection of books, people have established schools, hospitals, various organizations, and communities.

There is something to the fact that this collection of books has inspired countless people and societies. In fact, some have argued that the Bible influenced the writers of the United States Constitution as well as other national constitutions. The mere truth that the Bible has lasted this long and is still relevant to so many people is not complete or absolute proof that it comes from God, but it does speak volumes (no pun intended).

There is a story in the New Testament book of Acts that shares this sentiment. The religious authorities in Jerusalem were harassing the followers of Jesus and actually wanted to have them killed. A member of the Council, a Pharisee (a member of a Jewish sect) named Gamaliel, urged the authorities to leave the followers of Jesus alone. In Acts 5:38-39 he states, "'Here's my recommendation in this case: Distance yourselves from these men. Let them go! If their plan or activity is of human origin, it will end in ruin. If it originates with God, you won't be able to stop them. Instead, you would actually find yourselves fighting God!' The council was convinced by his reasoning." He was saying that what comes from God can't be stopped by human effort or even by time. Many sacred books from the ancient world have come and gone, but the Bible is still around. Why? Because something that comes from God cannot be diminished or eliminated simply because a few thousand years have passed.

The fact that there are over two billion Christians worldwide who adhere to (at least in theory) the principles of the Bible is also not hardcore proof. Nonetheless, it does give us an indication that the Bible transcends any one particular era and culture. Things that are worthwhile tend to last, and the Bible has done just that. Moreover, there is no indication that it will lose its influence and impact in the world in the coming years. For me, that is all the proof I need to at least read it and explore for myself to see if it has value and meaning.

Is the Bible Still Relevant?

Is the Bible still relevant today? In order to answer that question, it's important to address the hostility toward religion itself in the Western world. Ever since the Enlightenment (roughly the eighteenth century) we have seen more people view religion with skepticism for several reasons, the biggest being that much of it is not logical or rational and can't be proved. The Enlightenment period of scientific experimentation and philosophical exploration was an age when people were looking for proof of whether or not something was true. Religion, on the other hand, does not require proof, at least not in the same sense; it relies on faith. This led many to question whether religion was necessary at all. In spite of philosophers and scientists questioning religion, most people in the Western world were largely and proudly Christian. However, the doors of doubt and criticism were opened in that period and remained open.

Fast forward a few hundred years and things have changed slightly. While most people believe in a higher power, more and more people are stepping away from organized religion. A 2016 Pew Research poll shows that many people don't go to church because they want to stay open-minded and choose to make decisions for themselves.[3] For many young people spirituality seems to be the preference rather than organized religion. They believe that spirituality, as opposed to religion, allows more freedom and openness to new ideas. For me the concept of having spirituality without religion is a hard pill to swallow, being that the very concept of spirituality comes from religion. That is to say, we understand spirituality because it was birthed out of religion. It's like saying I don't like potatoes, but I love French Fries. Or I like steak but I don't like beef.

Spirituality, whether you like it or not, is deeply connected to religion. In my estimation you really can't separate the two because one comes out of the other. Look at it from this perspective: religion is how one practices one's spirituality. Those who claim no religion do so, from my vantage point, falsely because spirituality becomes their religion. The reason is that their spirituality is based on *something*, whether they want to admit it or not. More than likely it is based, in part, on whatever religious tradition they walked away from, what they are most familiar with, and/or whatever religious tradition is most common in their environment. The only difference is that they are only using the parts of religion that make the most sense to and have the most meaning for them. Well, that's me on my soapbox. Having said all of that, I do understand why so many people prefer spirituality, thinking they've left religion behind. It means having a relationship with God without the rituals, requirements, and worship obligations. It is freedom to pray and serve God as one chooses. This also means not having a sacred book, which can be hard to understand, as a guideline on how to live, which brings us back to the original question, is the Bible relevant today?

For many in the modern world the Bible has some very nice stories and even some inspirational phrases, but that's about it. There are stories about a large body of water parting, a little boy killing a giant that everyone else was afraid of, and a man being swallowed and then spit up by a big fish. For many, these stories and other miracles are hard to believe but filled with some sort of point even if we don't always grasp it. However, what becomes more troubling are the verses about commands to wipe out entire peoples, killing children, and a seemingly very angry and vengeful God. (I will talk about disturbing images in the Bible in another chapter.) This leads some to ask the question, "What kind of God would do all of this?" Perhaps that's why a lot of people today view the scriptures as a bunch of superstition or made-up stories that don't make sense.

What kind of God does that?

I've heard so many people say that they simply don't understand the Bible or believe the Bible. Yet much of the Western world is built upon the principles that we find in holy scripture. So the beginning of understanding the Bible is acknowledging that it is not easy to understand; it has some inconsistencies, some troubling parts, and some flat-out weird stuff. It is important to acknowledge that, because it helps, as it does with everything, to admit what you are feeling whenever embarking on a task. And the task here is to understand and even appreciate this series of collected writings we call the Bible.

I spent a few months in clinical pastoral education right after I finished seminary. This is hospital chaplaincy training for clergy. One of the things we were taught is that before we enter into any hospital room, it is vital that we assess how we are feeling. The reason is that how you feel affects how you act. And if you are aware of and acknowledge those feelings, you are better equipped to minister to the patient. It is the same way when reading the Bible. So I want to acknowledge what many people are feeling and thinking, that is, that the Bible doesn't always make sense. And feeling that way is okay.

Why Does It Matter?

I remember one time at the gym when, after my workout, I went to sit in the sauna for a while. I listened while several men talked about politics and current affairs. In the middle of the conversation, one of them said, "I believe in God but I have serious doubts about the Bible." Out of curiosity I asked him why he had doubts about the Bible, and he simply said, "Because it was written by man [humans]." We had a very interesting conversation after that. It was not a debate or confrontational in any form. We were both trying to understand the other person's position.

I reminded him that everything that we have has been written by humans, including all of our local, state, and national laws. Does that mean we should throw them out simply because they were written by mortals? I realize that there are unjust laws and serious problems with our judicial system, but for the most part the intent behind the laws is good. What makes all the difference is how those laws are understood and carried out. They must be executed with no partiality whatsoever. In the same manner, the Bible was written with the best intentions in mind. And even though there are some culturally disturbing parts, the general purpose of the book is good. What is most important is how we understand it and execute what the Bible is intended for. The reason it matters is that there are obvious helpful and important lessons we can learn from scripture. I believe that is why it has lasted from one generation to the next.

What Counts as Essential?

In all actuality, because of the complexity of the Bible, people have understood it in different ways over the centuries. That is the primary reason why we have so many different denominations. It is the reason why there are many issues that not all Christians see eye-to-eye on. And that's okay, because there are many things we do agree on. Take for example the issue of women in ministry. While there are many denominations that have been ordaining women for decades, there are others that don't see it as scriptural. It really depends on if your approach to scripture is literal, allegorical, or contextual. Those are terms we will explore later in the book.

There are active followers of Jesus who believe that to ordain women would violate the Bible and compromise the history of the Church. There are faithful disciples of Jesus who believe that ordaining women fits completely with the trajectory of and principles of scripture. Which group is Christian? Both, because our primary mandate is to follow Jesus. And if both sides believe that, it means that we all share some common values.

I think a fundamental question that every person who calls himself or herself Christian must answer is: "What are the essentials of the Christian faith?" In other words, what must every follower of Jesus believe in order to scripturally be counted as a disciple? Some have actually written books about the belief essentials of Christianity. However, in an effort to move us along, let's try to summarize it in a few paragraphs. That is to say, I will use the Twitter version rather than the Facebook version.

I want to lift of up two passages of scripture to help lay the foundation for what one ought to believe in order to be called Christian. The first is John 14:23, "Jesus answered, 'Whoever loves me will keep my word. My Father will love them, and we will come to them and make our home with them.'" I don't think anyone will argue against the notion that discipleship means loving Jesus and striving to obey what he commanded. Of course, Jesus taught many things, but there is only one, in particular, that is vital. We lift it up every Maundy Thursday, which is the day before Jesus was killed on a cross. Jesus says in John 13:34-35, "I give you a new commandment: Love each other. Just as I have loved you, so you also must love each other. This is how everyone will know that you are my disciples, when you love each other."

It seems to me that Jesus lays out what the necessary belief ought to be and that is to love him and love others the way he loves. That's what every Christian, regardless of whether they are theologically conservative, progressive, or moderate, should live. Everything else that we teach and believe might be extremely important but is not essential to salvation, if I understand John 3:16 correctly. Please don't mistake what I'm saying to suggest that beyond loving Jesus and loving like Jesus, you can believe whatever you want. Nothing could be further from the truth. Everything we believe beyond that helps inform our discipleship. However, if we are looking at what is absolutely necessary to believe, then it really does boil down to loving Jesus and loving like him. I would also add Romans 10:9, which teaches the importance of confessing and believing that Jesus is Lord and that he was raised from the dead.

However, there is deep disagreement over several issues. Many believe that if we accept certain beliefs, then we are denying the Bible. And for many that would be almost the same as denying God because the Bible contains God's plan of salvation through Jesus. Furthermore, to deny scripture would lead to a dangerous spiral downward into the pit of anything goes. Nevertheless, that argument leads to another debate altogether, and that is how we are to interpret the Bible.

Christians from the earliest times have approached the Bible differently. Some have read and continue to read it literally, some take an allegorical approach, still others view it from a contextual standpoint, and some mix and match those three approaches. That is another thing Christians don't agree on, but does one's approach to the Bible determine that person's Christianity or is it determined by one's willingness to strive to pattern one's life after Jesus Christ?

This means there are some issues that we as Christians will never agree on no matter how we interpret the Bible, but we all believe in the essential. That's where our conversation should start, and it ought to be the guiding principle of our discussions. I am fully aware that some feel hurt and excluded by some of the Church's stances on certain issues. I understand that and can only offer that I don't believe it is with malicious intent that many embrace some of the current positions held by different denominations and congregations. It is truly what some believe based on the Bible and their interpretation. Most Christians didn't *first* decide to condemn groups like women, parents with children out of wedlock, or divorcees, and *then* find scripture to justify their thinking, as was the case with the transatlantic slave trade.

It is not hard to see how some denominations and independent congregations came to their stance on women's ordination from their reading of 1 Corinthians 14:34, "The women should be quiet during the meeting. They are not allowed to talk. Instead, they need to get under control, just as the Law says."

Another source of disagreement among Christians, and there are many, is baptism. Many Christians believe in what is called a believer's baptism. This is the concept that in order to be brought into the Body of Christ, the Church, one must publicly profess her or his faith. That is to say, people must accept and verbalize for themselves their belief that Jesus died for our sins and was raised from the dead. Taking that understanding is quite biblical. After all, you can see throughout the book of Acts adults accepting Jesus and being baptized. On the other hand, you also see in the book of Acts someone accepting Jesus and then having their entire household baptized (Acts 16:15). This is why others in the Christian community practice infant baptism. This is where adults (parents or guardians) have young children brought into the life of the Church, children who are unable to speak for themselves. When such children reach a certain age when they are considered able to make their own decisions, they are confirmed after going through a confirmation class. Confirmation means they affirm what took place at their baptism and they then take the responsibility of their faith as their own.

To add to that debate, some believe that baptism is valid only when one is fully immersed in water. This is what we see in Matthew 3 when John, the relative of Jesus, baptized Jesus. However, some baptize by pouring or sprinkling water on the person. One biblical basis for this is found in Hebrews chapter 9, which gives an account of Moses (Old

Testament) sprinkling the blood of sacrificed animals on people who were viewed as ceremonially unclean, thus making them ceremonially clean. In the same manner when one is baptized the belief is that the water is a symbol of being spiritually cleansed.

Both believer's baptism and infant baptism are rooted in scripture, and a case for baptism by full immersion and sprinkling can both be made using scripture. So which one is right and which one is wrong? Or can they both be right based on how one approaches scripture? Furthermore, is the how or when of baptism an essential when it comes to Christian life? Some would argue yes, and others would disagree. We could go on and on about the different ways in which people understand scripture, but at some point we have to ask ourselves what is essential and what is nonessential to being a follower of Jesus.

You can look at the Constitution of the United States in some of the same ways as scripture, although the Constitution is not on the same level. There are varying opinions on certain statements and amendments. The Second Amendment is a perfect example. It actually says: "A well regulated Militia, being necessary to the security of a free State, the right of the people to keep and bear Arms, shall not be infringed." Some read that and say: "I have a right to buy any firearm that is legal." Others would cite the historical context, in which that amendment applies to state militias and not individuals. They would argue that the founding fathers never could have imagined the proliferation of guns we now see in the US. They would argue that the Second Amendment, with the mass production and ownership of the types of destructive guns we see today, has been taken out of context. The other side would argue that the Second Amendment says: "I have the right to own a gun, it does not say what kind nor does it say how many." Those two sides will probably never agree but both sides are reading the same Constitution.

Please know that I don't believe all these varying interpretations of scripture should ignite major conflict. It is simply a matter of belief and how one reads and interprets the Bible. Others outside of the Church might argue by saying: "Why would you bother reading the Bible if it brings that much confusion?" Others, who look to the Bible for answers but are simply confused by it, might wonder, "How do you interpret an ancient book in light of modern issues?"

Let me give a brief and overly simplistic review of why and how we have so many different Christian denominations who look to the Bible as the source of faith but still disagree. My hope is that doing so will shed light on the various ways people have read scripture throughout history.

In the early days of the Church there weren't different denominations. All followers of Christ belonged to one Church. In essence the same is true today. All believers, regardless of their denominational affiliation, belong to the same Universal Church. Ephesians 4:5 says, "There is one Lord, one faith, one baptism." However, the Church began to fracture when different schools with different perspectives emerged. Disputes arose that were political in nature as well as theological (related to ways we understand and talk about God). This led to what became known as the Great Schism, when the Eastern Church broke away from the Western Church in 1054. The Eastern Church became Eastern Orthodox and was headquartered in Constantinople (modern-day Istanbul) for hundreds of years. The Western Church became the Roman Catholic Church headquartered in Rome, and it is still there today.

In the sixteenth century people began protesting some of the practices of the Roman Catholic Church, and this eventually led to various Protestant (protest-ant) denominations. Many of these denominations have split from each other over disagreements regarding social issues such as slavery, polity (how a church is structured and organized), holiness, and most recently human sexuality. Denominations that have been fractured over these issues include but are not limited to Methodists, Baptists, Presbyterians, Lutherans, and Episcopalians. While these groups have split over what I would call non-essentials, they all still hold one thing in common, and that is the life, death, and resurrection of Jesus as the essential of our faith.

I said all of that to say that people understand the Bible differently. It has always been the case and it always will be. My only point on this issue is that as long as we hold fast to the essential of what the Bible teaches about faith, we are all still in the same boat.

What Exactly Is the Bible?

If you asked most people what the Bible is, they would probably respond by saying it is the sacred text for those who call themselves Christian. And they would be correct. But what exactly is the Bible? Before I can answer that I need to tell you what it is not. It is important to reiterate what I stated in chapter 1: the Bible is not a history book or science book. If you want to gain a good understanding of historical events, you should read a history book. If you want to understand the science of the universe, read a science book. That's not to say that the Bible and science don't go together, because I believe they do. In fact, I think they can complement each other. What we now know about astronomy, biology, and physics can actually help us expand our appreciation for the scriptures. The same can be said about history. Knowing history, in particular the time periods in which scripture takes place, can help us make sense of certain passages. Yes, science, history, and religion can go together, but they are not the same.

The Bible is a collection of books that tell the story of God's interaction with and involvement in the world through a particular people whom we know as the Jewish people. It is not a book about a bunch of perfectly holy people whose example we must follow. It is more about learning from their mistakes, confusion, selfishness, and idolatry, but also their faithfulness and love of God—not just what they did wrong but what also they did right. One thing that we can certainly learn from the people in the Bible is their unwavering commitment to make sense of life using God as the basis. Most importantly, when you read the Bible you should really focus on the relationship between Israel and God. That is to say, what are God's expectations, how does God respond to obedience and disobedience, and what plans does God have for God's people?

God is who God is, and God loves all creation, including you.

The Bible is important because it is the only book that contains God's plan for salvation—God's plan for us. It lays out God's reason for wanting to save humanity. It also shares why humanity needs to be saved in the first place and how, despite some desperate attempts, we cannot save ourselves.

III.

Why Do We Need to Be Saved?

One might ask, and rightfully so, "Why do we need to be saved in the first place, and what are we being saved from?" Well, to use a biblical term, it is because of sin. Sin can be defined as missing the mark. Following what God requires is how we hit the mark, but when we stray away from that we miss the mark. And what is that mark? It is nothing less than what is right and true. It is what will give us what the Bible calls an abundant life–a life characterized by love, peace, patience, kindness, gentleness, goodness, and self-control. We sin when we turn away from having that kind of life, the life that God intends for us–a life with God. The result of our sin is separating ourselves from God and the good God intends for all creation.

According to the Bible, sin also has consequences. "The wages that sin pays are death, but God's gift is eternal life in Christ Jesus our Lord" (Romans 6:23). In other words, the penalty for disobeying God is death. God is the source of life, so when we turn away, we turn away from life and we turn toward death, because there is no life apart from God. I know that sounds harsh, but because we are free to choose, we also face the very real consequences of our decisions. God will not force God's self on us. It's like a parent telling the child the consequences of breaking the rules of the house, which the parent pays for. Yes, in some ways we are like children. We don't know any better until we're taught. We all are guilty of choosing those things that are not of God. We are all guilty of putting our selfish desires before what is good for others, even if it is only once in a while. We are just prone to do it. We all miss the mark and continue to miss the mark set by God. Sometimes we even cause others to miss the mark. We just can't help ourselves, and that is the point.

It's easy to spot how human beings have missed the mark when we look at society. There is violence in city streets across the globe. We see oppression of people based on race, nationality, gender, and economic status. There is pay inequality for women, especially women of color. War is constant and genocide seems to be the norm. One could make the argument that humanity has done much more than miss the mark, we often shoot in the wrong direction altogether.

However, we don't need to look at the larger society to see how badly we have missed the mark. All we have to do is look in the mirror. If we are honest with ourselves, we see that we are all in need of being saved. If the truth be told, we are not always truthful to others or even to ourselves. We sometimes say hurtful things to people, even those we love. We are not always kind to others who are not like us. What makes it so bad is that we often do things we know we shouldn't do. And we sometimes hurt people emotionally without even knowing it. The list goes on and on. When we really examine society and ourselves, it is clear that we have made a mess of things; we have missed God's mark and are in need of being saved.

Why Does God Want to Save Us?

Let me say that if God wants something, then God accomplishes it. And God wants to save humanity. The reason why God wants to save human beings is quite simple yet profound.

God absolutely loves what God created. God created human beings as the pinnacle of God's creation. God's love for us is captured throughout scripture, in both Old and New Testaments. God loves us because love is who God is, and God demonstrates love to us in a variety of ways. It is as if God said to Godself, "I am love and want other creatures to experience love that knows no bounds. Therefore, I am going to create so that creation will know and feel the love that I AM."

It is actually God's love that allows us to have free will–the ability to choose between right and wrong. We are free to turn toward God or turn away from God. The Creator did not want us to be mere robots that cannot think and act on their own. If that were the case, we would never really understand the depths of God's love and we could not freely choose to love God or each other. How could we? All we would know is that we do whatever it is that we are programmed to do. How can a computer know that you love it when it is unable to think on its own? Of course, this excludes the movie *Her*, about a man who falls in love with his programming system. But in all seriousness God did not create us to be computers. We are free to love or not to love, and the very idea that God allows us the freedom to be and do what we want is a perfect example of love–even when that freedom leads us away from a relationship with God. It is that love that God has for humanity that makes God want to rescue us.

How Does God Save Us?

Many ancient civilizations believed in the practice of sacrifice. Civilizations such as those in areas that are now Japan, India, Greece, Egypt, North America, and South America sacrificed animals, people, and vegetation in an effort to please, appease, or bargain with their gods. The fact that various peoples around the globe, even with having no contact with each other, all felt the necessity to do the same thing speaks volumes. There must be something innate within us that moves us to believe that when we do wrong, we must do something to make up for the wrong that we do.

I truly believe that within every creature is the desire (known or unknown) to connect, strengthen a connection, or reconnect with their creator. It was the blood of animals and people that ancient civilizations believed would satisfy their god(s) and prevent them from having to deal with the consequences of angering their god(s). Why blood? Because life was in the blood. "Basic to both animal and human sacrifice is the recognition of blood as the sacred life force in man [humanity] and beast. Through the sacrifice–through the return of the sacred life revealed in the victim–the god lives, and, therefore, man and nature live."[4] That is to say, someone's or something's life blood was required in order for life to be sustained.

We see the same belief system in the Bible. In the Old Testament animal sacrifices were made as a way of paying the penalty for disobeying God, and the penalty was death. The animal's sacrifice was meant to serve as a substitute for the person's blood. As already mentioned, Romans 6:23 says, "The wages that sin pays are death, but God's gift is eternal life in Christ Jesus our Lord." Again, this idea was not unique to the Israelites but was common in antiquity.

For the New Testament the blood that Jesus shed on the cross was the final sacrifice made for all people. Simply put, when one disobeys God the punishment is death (eternal); and in order to pay for sin blood (life) is required. Jesus paid our penalty of eternal death with his blood. In doing so he became the perfect sacrifice to God for the past, present, and future sins of humanity. That's how much God loves us and that is how God saves us. This is also one way Christianity is different from all other religions. Christians believe that God Godself (that is, Jesus) paid the price for our sin. We do not earn it; we cannot match it; we do not deserve it. We are saved through the grace of God. God's gift of grace is freely given, no strings attached. This is what makes the Bible important. It explains why we need to be saved, why God wants to save us, and how God saves us.

Who Is Jesus and How Does He Fit In?

The foundation of Christianity is Jesus–his teachings, miracles, death on the cross, and resurrection from the grave. Most notable of all of Jesus's acts, of course, was the resurrection. Without the resurrection it is highly unlikely that the New Testament would have been written at all. The story of Jesus's return from the grave was shared verbally (most of the scripture was shared orally before it was ever written down) and eventually written so that it could stand the test of time. For those of the Jewish tradition, the Exodus is the central story of their faith. For Christians it is the resurrection of Jesus of Nazareth. That is why it is important, when trying to understand the Bible and the Christian faith, that you first understand who Jesus is. The claims made by and about Jesus are critical to who we are as his followers. While I can't prove beyond a shadow of a doubt everything about Jesus–it's a matter of faith–I will share some thoughts that I hope will help us have a clearer understanding of who Jesus is.

Is Jesus Really Who He Says He Is?

Looking at the life and times of Jesus of Nazareth, you find some seemingly outrageous claims. There is the claim that

Jesus made to a group of religious leaders that startled and even angered them. In John 10:30 Jesus declares that he and the Father (God) are one and the same. Then in John 14:9, responding to a question by one of his followers, Philip, Jesus professes that if you have laid eyes on him, then that means you have seen the Father (God). In essence what Jesus proclaims in those two statements as well as a few others is that he is equal with God. In fact, he even says that he is God. While debating with some of his many critics, in John 8:58 Jesus states that before Abraham existed, "I Am." Here Jesus uses God's name "Yahweh." Jesus's listeners react with terrified horror, because Jews believed if someone said the personal name of God, which is exactly what Jesus did, that person would be struck dead. What made that statement even more audacious is that it is the very way in which God, in the book of Exodus, tells Moses to refer to God–a story which would have been very familiar. If someone is going to make such a bold statement, most people will want some sort of proof. Apparently the fact that Jesus was not struck dead was not enough.

Today some people believe Jesus to be a prophet, others a great teacher, and still others a good moral leader, just not God in the flesh. To say Jesus is God is a different story altogether. People can believe whatever they want about Jesus. It is completely fine to view Jesus as a great teacher, but Jesus actually claimed to be more than that. He professed that he was the beginning and the end. That is a title that only the creator of the universe could have. In order for the Bible, in particular the New Testament, to truly make sense you have to come to grips with who Jesus says he is.

Examining what Jesus did, many would say that he performed many great deeds. He gave sight to the blind, healed the sick, and even raised people from the dead. He walked on water and cast demons out of those who were possessed. Isn't that proof enough right there? Sure, he had some fantastic miracles, so shouldn't that be an indicator that he is who he says? I think those are definite indicators that he is someone special; however, there are claims of others outside and within the biblical narrative doing some of the same things. I could try to produce more evidence by sharing that he was believed to be without sin. He is the only person to walk the face of the earth, purportedly, without doing wrong. But then again, how can that be proved? The fact that people say Jesus was sinless definitely means something, but is that enough proof?

If God were to visit us on earth, you would expect God to be blameless and work miracles, but some would still want more proof. It is hard to deny that Jesus had power, and the Gospels record his great and wondrous works. There are even documents outside of the biblical account that Jesus did many of those things. But you would think that God would have also left the world some sort of great teaching in addition to the deeds. As you look to see what new philosophies Jesus brought to the world, you will discover that there isn't much that he taught that hadn't already been shared. Sure, he elaborated further on previous teachings. He even reinterpreted some things to bring a greater meaning to them. On top of all that, he gave the world a new commandment of loving others the way he loves. But the fact still remains that there isn't a long list of teachings to which he alone can claim authorship. Maybe that's because, as we learn in the Old Testament book of Ecclesiastes, there isn't anything new under the sun. Whatever the reason, there just isn't a lot, in terms of unique thought, that separates Jesus from other great teachers in world history.

Nonetheless, when you consider his new perspective on old teachings, his miracles, and of course his resurrection, he is a unique figure. Not to mention how he went against the norms of the day by including women in his ministry, eating in the homes of people considered sinners, and forgiving people of their wrongdoing. He broke the custom of his era in that he engaged in conversations with other ethnic groups, for example the Samaritans, who were hated and considered "half-breeds" by Jews. Jesus actually broke tradition when he made a member of a different ethnic group the hero in one of his parables, what many call the Parable of the Good Samaritan, found in Luke 10:25-37. In addition, the resurrection is no small accomplishment to say the least. For many, the fact that countless people claimed to have seen Jesus after he had been crucified is enough proof. But for now, I want to move beyond the resurrection to a teaching of Jesus that was especially revolutionary.

Jesus was unique.

Matthew 5:38-45 says,

> You have heard that it was said, *An eye for an eye and a tooth for a tooth*. But I say to you that you must not oppose those who want to hurt you. If people slap you on your right cheek, you must turn the left cheek to them as well. When they wish to haul you to court and take your shirt, let them have your coat too. When they force you to go one mile, go with them two. Give to those who ask, and don't refuse those who wish to borrow from you.
>
> You have heard that it was said, *You must love your neighbor* and hate your enemy. But I say to you, love your enemies and pray for those who harass you so that you will be acting as children of your Father who

> is in heaven. He makes the sun rise on both the evil and the good and sends rain on both the righteous and the unrighteous.

Jesus urged his followers to love and pray for people who hate, despise, and mistreat them. That would have been unheard of for the people Jesus first spoke the words to. Jesus even told his followers to turn the other cheek once someone strikes them. It's not logical; it makes no sense whatsoever to wish the well-being of people who want to do you harm. There isn't much teaching around a concept like this from others. In fact, many of the great thinkers would say that does not make much sense. You can be kind to those you don't like, but you want me to ask God to bless them!? The world hadn't heard such a teaching before. The followers of Jesus, I would imagine, were shocked. It is perhaps the most radical teaching ever uttered.

Looking at some of the other great and profound historical teachers you might find something similar but not the same. Let's look at some of the great teachers who came before Jesus. The great Chinese philosopher Confucius, who lived five hundred years before Jesus, developed a system of beliefs for Chinese people. Confucius taught that justice is the proper response to cruelty.[5] You repay your enemies with justice, but you don't pray for them. The ancient Greek philosopher Socrates taught that you should not retaliate when someone does you harm. He believed that retaliation was a form of injustice. However, he did not teach that one should love one's enemies.[6]

Siddhartha Gautama, known to most of us as the Buddha, also lived centuries before Jesus, and had his own perspective. He was a pacifist, meaning he did not believe in violence. He taught something similar to Jesus in saying that loving-kindness (friendliness) ought to be shown to others including enemies. However, what he did not teach was to pray for your enemies. Even Moses, the one who led the Hebrews out of Egyptian bondage and received the Ten Commandments from God, did not teach the concept of praying for and loving your enemies. In fact, Moses taught retaliation. In Leviticus 24:17-20 it says,

> If anyone kills another person, they must be executed. Someone who kills an animal may make amends for it: a life for a life. If someone injures a fellow citizen, they will suffer the same injury they inflicted: broken bone for broken bone, an eye for an eye, a tooth for a tooth. The same injury the person inflicted on the other will be inflicted on them.

The point is that Jesus's teachings on how to treat enemies were unique. Christians may perhaps consider this concept of praying for and loving your enemy to be an ideal that can only be fully realized in some other perfect world and is rarely practiced in this one. It is much easier to teach this concept than to live it out. You might even ask the question, "Did Jesus put this teaching into practice?"

I'm glad you asked that question. Jesus had enemies in the form of the religious leaders of his day. If ever there was a group that despised an individual, it was the religious leaders in first-century Palestine. They despised him with a passion. Simply put, they wanted him dead. He taught things that they believed went against Jewish law. He made claims about himself that they believed were blasphemous. They were also afraid that Jesus would stir people up such that the Roman overlords would go on a killing rampage, which had happened before. Jesus was worthy only of one thing and that was death. You see, when Jesus came on the scene crowds of people began to flock to the countryside and villages to hear him speak. That took a lot of attention away from the religious leaders, who were used to being considered the experts. Plus, Jesus chastised them for many of their hypocritical practices.

Consequently, these religious leaders plotted and planned to come up with ways to catch Jesus and kill him. They met and discussed ideas and finally found a traitor among the followers of Jesus who would give him up. They even went out and found people who brought false accusations against Jesus and influenced the gathered crowd to ask for a man named Barabbas to be released from prison and have Jesus executed in his stead. They finally got their wish and Jesus was convicted and sentenced to death. Before he died, Jesus was humiliated, beaten, tortured, laughed at, mocked, and even made to carry the very cross he would be executed on.

I envision the religious leaders giving each other high fives as his hands were being nailed to the cross. It was a great day for those who wanted Jesus dead. As their enemy was hanging on the cross about to die, Jesus did not suggest any type of retaliation. He did not demand that his enemies be brought to justice. He did not demand their blood as the Old Testament law commands. Instead Jesus looked at those who hated him and he uttered the words that hold significance beyond understanding. In Luke 23:34 he says, "Father, forgive them, for they don't know what they're doing." Right there in the midst of his pain and agony he put into practice the most revolutionary teaching ever uttered on earth. He asked God to forgive the people who had had him falsely arrested, tortured, and sentenced to death. For many that is pretty good evidence that he is who he says he is.

For the Christian, knowing who Jesus is, what he taught, and what he stood for is paramount in finding meaning in the written account of God's interaction with the world. The Bible gives evidence that Jesus is who he claims he is. Because Jesus is the Word of God, knowing who he is can help us understand scripture better.

Why Do We Need Jesus?

Some might ask, and rightfully so, "Why do we have to be saved through Jesus? Why can't we save ourselves?" The best way to answer those questions is by stating that God is a perfect being, meaning God makes no mistakes and God always does the right and most loving thing possible given the circumstances people in their own limited, self-serving ways create.

There is a phrase among believers that says, "God can do everything except fail." To be blunt, if God does something that means it is not wrong. If God does anything that means it is right and perfect. Humans, on the other hand, make mistakes constantly; we do the wrong things sometimes almost instinctively. Sometimes we know we are making mistakes and other times we aren't even aware of it. We simply don't know what we don't know. And there are times we do the wrong thing simply because we are curious. If you look at the story of Adam and Eve in the book of Genesis, they were told that they could eat from any tree in the Garden of Eden with the exception of the tree of knowledge of good and evil. I believe they ate from the tree out of curiosity. If you tell someone they can't do something, then their curiosity tends to lead them to ask why, which in turn could lead them to find out for themselves.

There are other times we do wrong because we don't seem to be strong enough to resist temptation. That is to say, our willpower is weak. Have you ever eaten more chocolate cake and ice cream than you intended to? We've all been there. It is because we are not resilient enough to resist the strong call of the cake and ice cream. The Apostle Paul talks about this as he writes to the church that was meeting in Rome. He talks about how he keeps on doing the things that he doesn't want to do. He says in Romans 7:14-17,

> We know that the Law is spiritual, but I'm made of flesh and blood, and I'm sold as a slave to sin. I don't know what I'm doing, because I don't do what I want to do. Instead, I do the thing that I hate. But if I'm doing the thing that I don't want to do, I'm agreeing that the Law is right. But now I'm not the one doing it anymore. Instead, it's sin that lives in me.

Why do we do this? Because we are sinful creatures. Or, to say it a better way, because we are not perfect like God is perfect. We can too easily see ourselves as the center of the universe, which is necessary for infants but not for mature people. We sin sometimes knowingly and sometimes we sin without really knowing it. Part of the reason for our sin is because, as much as human beings know, there is infinitely more we don't know. There are things we now know that centuries ago they didn't. For example, years ago people did not understand the concept of germs and the importance of washing hands. Even when the Hungarian physician and scientist Ignaz Semmelweis first introduced the concept of washing hands to prevent the spread of disease, people didn't truly grasp the concept. It would not be until French scientist Louis Pasteur built upon the work of Semmelweis that people finally embraced it and then only reluctantly. We now know just how important hand-washing is, especially in this coronavirus era. Then again, there are things we are doing today that we will discover, years from now, are harmful. We are imperfect beings morally, intellectually, and physically.

The problem with being imperfect is that God does not accept anything that is not perfect morally, intellectually, or physically. I know that may seem strange, but think about it like those Flonase commercials. They show images of things like a dog with half a haircut or a table with dust on one half of it and none on the other side. The voice in the commercial says, "You wouldn't accept an incomplete job from anyone else, so why accept it from your allergy pills?" God doesn't accept anything less than perfection from Godself, so why would God accept it from anyone or anything else?

Regarding the ancient practice of sacrifice, the Bible teaches that people could not bring an animal to God that had any type of defect. After all, God gave and gives us God's best, so why would God lower God's standards all of a sudden? That being the case it takes some sort of mediation for us to be in a right relationship with God–a pure, blameless something or someone who can stand in for us because we can't be good enough on our own merit. It doesn't matter if you meet society's standards of being a good person or not, no one is without sin. We have all done things that go contrary to what God requires and expects. And God does not allow tainted things or people in God's presence. That's why we can't save ourselves. It would be like using a dirty rag to clean an even dirtier table.

Therefore, in order to truly be made right with God, humanity needed a perfect sacrifice, a sacrifice that would be final and for every generation. But this sacrifice had to be without fault and blemishes itself. The New Testament teaches us that Jesus is a person who did everything that lines up with God's will. First Peter 2:22 teaches that Jesus was sinless: "He committed no sin, nor did he ever speak in ways meant to deceive." Colossians 1:21-23 explains it well:

> Once you were alienated from God and you were enemies with him in your minds, which was shown by your evil actions. But now he has reconciled you by his physical body through death, to present you before God as a people who are holy, faultless, and without blame. But you need to remain well established and rooted in faith and not shift away from the hope given in the good news that you heard. This message has been preached throughout all creation under heaven. And I, Paul, became a servant of this good news.

This suggests that we are estranged from God because of our behavior. Even those who are considered good people are estranged. But we have been reunited with God because of the selfless and sacrificial act of Jesus on the cross. Jesus is free from sin and perfect in thought, deed, and words, and that makes him not just an acceptable sacrifice for the world but the best and only acceptable sacrifice for all people for all time.

IV.

How Should We Interpret the Bible?

In the movie *Jaws*, because a great white shark is terrorizing New England coastal waters, a crew made up of the sheriff of the town, a shark hunter, and a marine biologist sets sail to kill this giant predator. While the sheriff is throwing chum–bait–into the sea, the shark's terrible head breaks the water. The sheriff is shocked and begins backing away. In a moment of terror he says to the captain, "You're gonna need a bigger boat." When I think of how various groups understand scripture, it seems as though we have a big boat. That is to say there are many ways to interpret scripture. There are those who hold positions that can be considered liberal, moderate like myself, conservative, and in between.

Although Christians all belong to the same family, there's a lot of disagreement. I'm not sure that our disagreement is a bad thing. God is so big that not one person or group can really comprehend all that God is as revealed through scripture. To use the image from chapter 1, looking at God through the lens of scripture is like looking at a large building that stretches several blocks. Where you are standing around the building will determine what you see. Someone looking at a building can see something completely different from what someone else looking at the exact same building sees. Which one is right and which one is wrong? The reality is that both are right if they are both looking at the building. That's what's happening with the Bible. We have different people standing in different places in life in different contexts with different histories.

Whether we acknowledge it or not, our personal tracks in life shape how we understand scripture. What I mean by that is we are all shaped by our race, nationality, upbringing, friends, education, family, and religious background or lack thereof. Those factors determine where we stand when it comes to scripture. So it's easy to see how people can interpret and understand scripture differently. And to me that's okay as long as we are looking at the same building/Bible.

What deters people from reading the Bible and causes disagreement and confusion is when people try to convince someone who's standing in a different place in life to read scripture like them. That's scary because it's like trying to convince someone who is standing on the other side of the building that what they might be looking at is wrong, while trying to assure them that what I see on my side is what's right and the only way of looking at the building. Being told that you have to read scripture from a perspective that is opposite to yours is a major way that you can come to think the Bible is irrelevant or you can't understand it, much less believe it.

Why So Many Translations?

There are several reasons why there are so many different translations of the Bible. First, it is good to note that there are some words in Hebrew, the language in which much of the Old Testament was written, and Greek, the language of the New Testament, that don't have equivalents in the English language. As a result, translators take different approaches in converting those words to English. Some take the approach of trying, as much as possible, to find the English word that most closely matches the Hebrew or Greek. Even those who take this approach may come up with different English words, because they differ on which word fits best. Another approach that leads to various translations is, rather than trying to match it word for word, matching thought for thought. This philosophy tries to take the spirit of the Hebrew and Greek texts and find the best way of expressing it in English. Still another approach in translating the Bible is that translators try to find the best word as well as capturing the spirit of the text. Then there are those Bibles that are more of an interpretation than a translation. The difference between the two is that an interpretation seeks to explain it and a translation is simply deciphering one language to another; although there is always a degree of interpretation. And sometimes scholars or even novelists simply paraphrase what they think the Bible says. This is why we have so many different translations, yet for all these different approaches, people still have difficulty understanding the Bible.

What Are Some Methods for Interpreting the Bible?

Through the years there have been various ways of interpreting the Bible. The branch of knowledge that deals with interpretation is called "hermeneutics," and depending on one's perspective, one's approach to understanding scripture will differ. But regardless of the method of interpretation, the overall purpose is to find value and meaning so that one can come to know the truth of God.

Literal Interpretation

One of the most obvious ways of approaching scripture is literal interpretation. In this sense, you are looking to find the plain meaning. When one uses the literal approach, you are not searching for symbols, metaphors, or allegories. It is taking the words in their obvious and traditional sense, to you, and understanding it as-is. People who use this approach to interpret scripture might say something like, "The Bible means what it says." The good thing about this approach is that it avoids the potential of distorting or inflating the meaning behind certain stories. The disadvantage of this approach is that the Bible is literally filled with symbols, metaphors, and hyperbole, which can make understanding it problematic when taking a literal approach.

Allegorical Method

The allegorical approach to scripture means you are looking for a deeper meaning behind what is obvious. Those who employ this method believe that there are multiple levels of meaning in scripture. Some have even called this particular technique the mystic or spiritual interpretation of the Bible. That is to say, there is a more profound implication beyond the people, places, and things in the story. Literalists will quickly point out that this method of interpretation can easily mislead your understanding of what the scripture actually means. However, the advantage of this approach is that God truly is multifaceted and is much more profound than we can possibly imagine. Stated another way, there is more to God and God's Word than meets the eye.

Historical Method

Another method of interpreting the Bible is using a historical approach. This technique evaluates the historical setting in which a passage of scripture was written. What was happening to the people for whom the text was originally intended? What euphemisms, customs, worldviews, and even scientific understandings were prevalent during the time of the writing? The historical method strives to separate the culture of the day from what God requires. A perfect example of that is how men, especially men of means, had multiple wives. A historical approach might say the Bible permits polygamy; however, this was never God's intent. It was simply the custom of the time. The danger of the historical method is that it is easy to treat the Bible as if it is just another literary document and not the God-inspired work that it is.

Moral Method

The moral or topological method of interpretation starts with the notion that the Bible is a book designed to teach us how to live morally. It contends that everything written in scripture was meant to teach us a lesson. In this sense the Bible shares with us what we should and should not do. In short the Bible is sort of a rule book for conduct and faith.

Hermeneutic of Suspicion

There are some other ways in which people interpret scripture, such as using what is called a "hermeneutic of suspicion." With this method, which is one that I favor, the modern reader takes into account how certain understandings of the Bible have been used by the powerful to oppress the weak and disadvantaged; for example, the Bible has been used to take advantage of women and minorities. You can see the merit of this method of interpretation. In short, one using this method does not necessarily trust the typical and historical way in which texts have been understood, in fear that one might be affirming unhealthy stereotypes. The hermeneutic of suspicion takes the stance that for centuries scholars, pastors, and laity have done more eisegesis than exegesis for the purpose of maintaining the status quo. That is, some people interpret the Bible in a way that confirms their own biases, prejudices, and presuppositions, rather than trying to discern what God is trying to say more objectively. All of this just goes to show you that, while the Bible might have meaning to diverse groups, we don't all read it the same way.

An Example

Let's take a brief overview of how these various methods would approach a particular text or story. Genesis chapter 3 is perhaps a perfect story to understand the many styles of interpretation. But first, take a Bible and read Genesis chapter 3. This is the story of Adam and Eve eating from the tree.

Using the literal approach to scripture, someone would say that after God created everything, including man and then woman, God informed them that they were free to enjoy everything in the Garden of Eden except one tree. Eve, after being coaxed by the serpent, convinced Adam to break God's commandment by eating from the tree of knowing good and evil. As a result of their disobedience Adam and Eve were escorted out of the garden and forbidden to ever return. Before they left, however, God clothed them and told Adam that his punishment would be having to work the land to eat and it would not be easy. Eve's punishment would be pain during childbirth. Human beings would never get to live in the Garden of Eden again. This interpretation follows the explanation of the story line.

The allegorical interpretation might suggest that God did not create a male and then a female but created a person. It could be understood that the word "man" really implies humankind, of which there are two kinds, men and women. The story of Adam and Eve, at its core, isn't a story of a man and a woman living in a literal beautiful garden but a story of men and women living in a perfect society that God created.

This society was loving, peaceful, and chaos free until men and women began doing things that disrupted the order of things. As a result of their harmful behavior, this society once characterized by harmony was disrupted and eventually disbanded. Ever since that time humanity has struggled to recreate, with God's help, that utopic civilization.

The historical approach to this story is not so simple. One using this approach might point out that this story is probably not historically accurate. We don't have any tangible evidence to confirm that Adam and Eve or the Garden of Eden ever existed. This seemingly single story is composed of a number of stories from various ancient cultures that had been passed down from one generation to the next and molded into this account. The biblical authors weren't necessarily trying to explain exactly how humanity and the various peoples of the earth came into existence. Because, frankly, Genesis fails to do that. The real point of the authors is that God created everything and is creation's ultimate ruler.

The moral method of understanding the story of Adam and Eve is direct. It is about obedience and disobedience. God gave them rules to follow and they blatantly defied God. The moral of the story is that when you do what God requires, then you can live in a state of abundance, harmony, and perfection. However, when you disobey God, you lose the blessings that God intends for you and must reap the consequences of your actions.

Those approaching Genesis 3 from a hermeneutic of suspicion might begin by asking how this story has been used to reduce women to second-class citizens. Some have used the text to suggest the frailty and weak-mindedness of women, because Eve was the one that the serpent talked into eating from the tree. She was the one who was not strong enough to resist the temptation of the serpent. However, this view fails to recognize or fully acknowledge that regardless of who was first, both of them ate from the tree.

Furthermore, it has been suggested that God told *Adam* not to eat from the tree, not Eve. Genesis 2:15-17 implies that the man was alone when God gave the instructions. Since the text says "he" and does not mention "she," the reader can assume that Eve was not present when God communicated this law. Either way, the bottom line is that both of them disobeyed God. Historically Eve, and by extension all women, has often been held to be the one most responsible for sin entering the world, but using a hermeneutic of suspicion might actually suggest the opposite.

Looking at the Old Testament Through the Lens of the New Testament

Christians typically look at the stories of the Old Testament through the lens of the New Testament, which includes the life, death, and resurrection of Jesus. The New Testament book of 1 Timothy also seeks to explain what happened in Genesis. In 2:14 it says, "Adam wasn't deceived, but rather his wife became the one who stepped over the line because she was completely deceived." This suggests that Adam was fully aware that he was disobeying God, while Eve was only tricked. That is to say, the woman sinned unknowingly while the man sinned knowingly. I think most would contend that doing wrong when you know it's wrong is more disturbing than doing wrong without knowledge that what you are doing is wrong. Thus Adam, not Eve, seems to be the real culprit.

All of these interpretative methods simply show us that there are many ways to approach scripture. Which way is best? All of them have their pros and cons, but it really boils down to what you feel comfortable with. Each one can be effective in certain circumstances, and frankly most people use a combination of all of them. The idea is that we use these methods as tools to open the scripture for our edification and to build up the entire body of Christian believers. In spite of the different approaches, each method can still lead to some common conclusions. What each method of interpreting the story of Adam and Even teaches is that humanity is not what it was intended to be; we fell into being less than we can and should be. Our relationship with God was severed because we didn't follow the rules God had put in place. As a result of that fall, God spends the rest of the Bible working to repair the broken relationship with humanity.

What about Disturbing Passages of Scripture?

One of the many things that trouble people about the Bible is that there are very disturbing images and stories. These sections are so alarming that it moves people to ask why these stories are in the Bible in the first place. There is the story in Genesis 19 where Lot offers his daughters to be sexually violated by an angry mob. Then there is King David, who, in 2 Samuel chapter 11, has Uriah killed so that he can marry Uriah's wife, Bathsheba, whom he has already impregnated. Wasn't David supposed to be a man of God? Why is David considered Israel's ideal king when he had so many flaws? He did and said absolutely nothing when his daughter Tamar was raped by her half-brother Amnon, David's son (2 Samuel 13). Perhaps the most disturbing image in scripture is found in Psalm 137:9, "A blessing on the one who seizes your children and smashes them against the rock!" What? Are you serious? How can something like this and the many other upsetting scriptures be in the Bible?

Things Were Different

While many people may never embrace these stories there is a point to them. First, it is important to reiterate what was stated earlier about the historical setting. These stories were written in a different time period in a completely different culture. Things were done completely differently than they are today. And it was written for people who would be very familiar with the customs from which the authors draw to tell the story. Think of it like this: there are things we do in the United States that are very strange to people who live in other parts of the world with a different culture and vice versa. One of the unusual things practiced in the United States and in a few other places is tipping. There are some countries where it is not required or expected. In those places a service fee is already included in the bill. Another American practice that might seem weird in other places is serving ice-cold drinks. Unless you ask otherwise, here in the States, a restaurant will more than likely give you plenty of ice in your drink. On the other hand, in other countries you won't get ice and the drink may be room temperature or slightly chilled. That was something I had a hard time adjusting to my first time overseas.

I said all of that to say there are different customs in different places.

The People of the Bible Were Mostly Like Us

Second, we often view the heroes of the Bible like Noah, Moses, David, and others as somehow being superhuman beings with extraordinary ethical powers. The truth of the matter is they were regular human beings with flaws, just like you and me. God did not give them any special abilities that are unavailable to us today. The remarkable thing we can learn from the stories of these biblical characters is that they made huge mistakes and God still used them to accomplish remarkable things. The same is true for us today. We all have lapses in judgment from time to time, yet God will still use you and me to accomplish God's purposes if we make ourselves available.

The Bible Uses Hyperbole as a Storytelling Device

The Bible, like a lot of important literature, is full of hyperbole. Now, please don't take that as if I am trying to devalue the importance of the Bible. I believe it is the most important document we have. And it is because it is so important that I am convinced we should know how to approach it when we read it. Hyperbole is a tool used by biblical writers to emphasize an important point or lesson. The use of exaggerated language and images captures the reader's attention, leading them to search out the intended message of the story–lessons that can easily be lost if we forget that we today are not the original intended audience. So keep in mind that many of the disturbing images and stories we read are exaggerated forms of what actually happened, and they are told in this way so that it will intrigue the reader to pay close attention.

Tragedy Was and Is Real

While some of the stories are straightforward and others use hyperbole, still others may be historically and tragically accurate. I know that might be problematic for some people; however, human life is full of trouble. As long as you have men and women, there is the potential for ugliness and mean-spiritedness to come out. That's something that the story of Adam and Eve is meant to teach us. But remember, the Bible is not so much the story of human beings as it is the story of God. It is told from the perspective of flawed individuals who are doing their best to decipher what they believe

God is leading them to do in the context of their culture. So it is also fair to ask, might they have been wrong or perhaps limited in their understanding?

How Should We Read the Bible Today?

One mistake many Christians make is that we read a single verse or chapter and then make universal claims based on that isolated text. Some call this reading in a vacuum. Clearly this should not be done, because the Bible was not written in a vacuum. What I mean by this is looking at one passage of scripture in order to understand a subject but not reading it in context with other scriptures on the same subject. For example, look at Psalm 29:2, "Give to the LORD the glory due his name! Bow down to the LORD in holy splendor!" Here we have a view of giving God glory as in some form of audible praise. But if you read 2 Chronicles 7:1, "As soon as Solomon finished praying, fire came down from heaven and consumed the entirely burned offering and the sacrifices, while the LORD's glory filled the temple," this text talks about God's glory filling the temple. In this sense the word "glory" is used to describe God's magnificent presence. However, when you read Romans 3:23, "All have sinned and fall short of God's glory," this text refers to God's glory as a standard by which our actions are measured.

To understand the various parts of the Bible, you need to study all of it.

If you read any of those texts by itself without trying to understand it in context with others you could possibly close the Bible with an incomplete understanding of what God's glory actually is. There are so many other examples of this throughout the Bible. How can you understand what Zion is by reading one passage alone when it is mentioned over 150 times throughout scripture? That's why it is important to not read any one scripture in isolation with the thought that each passage stands alone. It is for that reason one should not read scripture in a vacuum. Furthermore, to get an even truer sense of how the entirety of scripture develops, one needs to read and study all of it.

In the same sense if you start with Genesis and go all the way to Revelation, you see the evolution of the concept of hell. The way people understood what happens at death has changed over the millennia. For most Christians, hell is the place of eternal punishment. However, in some translations of the Bible, the word "hell" is rarely used. Instead, we see the word "Sheol," which was understood as the place of the dead. Early on in scripture there appears to be no clear concept of people being reprimanded forever in a place of torment.

Ancient peoples of the Bible believed that when you died, you went to the place of the dead. So the thought was that there is a place for living souls (earth) and a place for the nonliving souls (usually under the earth). By the time we get to the New Testament, however, the concept of a place of punishment or damnation was established. Whether one believes that hell is symbolic, literal, temporary, or permanent, you cannot arrive at the true meaning of hell by reading one or two passages of scripture about it. The best way to truly grasp a biblical concept is to explore the trajectory of scripture.

Where Is the Bible Trying to Take Us?

It's not so much where all of the authors are leading us as it is how the Holy Spirit works through the writers to establish some sort of path. I know the books within the Bible were written during different periods. I know that the authors had no idea that thousands of years later we would hold these sixty-six books to be the sacred writings about God. However, because we believe that scripture has been given by God, it makes sense that God had a plan all along. It doesn't really matter if the authors knew or believed this, because God can use us to do something without us knowing exactly what we've done.

Case in point, I've preached sermons before with a specific theme and intended message only to have someone tell me afterward that they got something else out of it. I used to think to myself, "That's not at all what the sermon was about." I say that I used to do that because I have come to the realization that God can use me to speak to someone about something specific they are going through. I remember one time when a woman came up to me after I preached. She was crying. She said she needed that message because of what she was dealing with regarding her family. As she explained the situation to me, I could see that my message didn't deal with that at all. However, God took my intent and used my words to speak directly to someone in need.

The point to all of this is to say that even if the authors were only writing to a specific audience with a specific context, God used it and uses it to accomplish much more. God is using these sixty-six books written by different authors under different circumstances to accomplish a purpose. One purpose is for certain themes to echo throughout scripture so that they resonate and stay with us.

If you look at the entirety of scripture, you can see there are a few common principles and at least one dominant theme. From the book of Genesis to the book of Revelation there is something that continues to be revealed over and over again, and that is God's desire to save humanity. I know, for many Christians, when we hear the words "saved" and "salvation," we think of being rescued from the penalty of sin, which is eternal death. However, salvation is more than just an afterlife experience; God intends that we enter God's kingdom now, in this life, even though it is only a foretaste of what will come. And while God's ultimate salvation is found through Jesus Christ, God has been saving us since the beginning of God's recorded story–the Bible. Salvation means to be rescued from some sort of danger or harm, and that danger can be physical, emotional, social, psychological, or spiritual.

We find God's first act of saving humanity in Genesis chapter 3. When Adam and Eve disobeyed God by eating from the tree of the knowledge of good and evil, God began God's saving action. Once Adam and Even realized they were naked, they felt ashamed and grabbed some fig leaves to cover themselves, but God rescued them from their shame by providing real clothes. God did not kill them for disobedience, though he did exile them. But even in exile, they would have other opportunities for reconciliation with God.

God's acts of saving humanity can be seen throughout Genesis in the stories of Noah and the flood, where God rescued the earth from corruption and put his "bow"–the rainbow–in the sky as a sign of peace. God then made a covenant, a contract, with Abraham in an effort to save all peoples through the descendants of him and his wife, Sarah. There are many other examples throughout the Bible where God saves and rescues people from physical, social, emotional, and ultimately spiritual harm and oppression.

Looking at the entire Bible, it can be summed up in three major events: the Exodus, Babylonian Exile, and the Resurrection. Each of these events underscores God's desire to save us and restore a right relationship with us. The book of Exodus shares the story of the Hebrews in Egyptian bondage. This story begins with Abraham's grandson Jacob and Jacob's twelve sons. Out of jealousy, the favorite son, Joseph, is sold into slavery by his brothers and taken to Egypt. Through a series of remarkable events, Joseph ends up being a top administrator in Pharaoh's court. Then comes a terrible drought, and those brothers who had hated Joseph end up in Pharaoh's court in front of Joseph, who they don't recognize, seeking food to ward off starvation. In another remarkable set of events, Joseph is reconciled with his brothers, then saves his father, brothers, and their families by inviting them to live in Egypt, the land of plenty. And all seems to end happily with them living well. But later a new Pharaoh of Egypt comes to power, one who does not know Joseph. That Pharaoh then decides to enslave Jacob's descendants, and they are forced to work and live at the pleasure of the Egyptians. For hundreds of years, these Hebrews cry out to the Lord. God hears their cry and responds by sending a deliverer in the person of Moses. Through Moses's leadership, God brings the Hebrews out of slavery in a miraculous fashion and gives them the Promised Land.

The next major event in the Bible is also found in the Old Testament. Second Kings tells the story of the siege of Jerusalem. Because of the people's sin, King Nebuchadnezzar leads the Babylonians, their enemy, into Jerusalem by destroying the protective wall around the city and the sacred Temple. Nebuchadnezzar carries off the prominent citizens from Jerusalem and forces them to live in exile in Babylon, leaving behind the poorest inhabitants to eke out an existence in the rubble. Eventually, after decades, the Jews are released from Babylon, set free to go home, rebuild the Temple, and get on with worshipping God as the people of God.

The other major event in the Bible is found in the New Testament. The story is recorded in the books of Matthew, Mark, Luke, and John. This event is most significant for Christians, and arguably it is the most important event in world history. I am referring to the resurrection of Jesus. Jesus was executed by the Romans because of charges brought against him by Jewish religious leaders. Jesus was killed and placed in a grave, but he did not stay there. His resurrection, for Christians, is a symbol of being set free from the confines of sin and death. This of course was all part of God's plan to save humanity from sin through the sacrificial act of Jesus.

When you read the Bible, most of it describes happenings leading up to one of these events, describes one of the three events directly, or explains the results of these events. In essence, the Bible is about what happened before, during, and after the Egyptian exodus, Babylonian exile, and the resurrection of Jesus. Those three events have one common theme, and that is deliverance, or as many prefer to say, liberation. The Hebrews–who later became the Jewish nation–were set free from Egyptian bondage and later released from Babylonian captivity. The liberation that Jesus provides is from the power of sin and death.

God wants us to live in response-able freedom.

Through the lens of the theme of liberation, we can see that God opposes oppressive structures and desires freedom for everyone, whether from psychological, physical, social, or spiritual persecution. This way of reading the Bible is a tool that I find helps make its stories understandable. God desires us to live in freedom. But freedom also carries responsibilities to love God, each other, ourselves, and our enemies. God wants us to be able to respond with truth and grace. As a result, when trying to comprehend a passage of scripture, especially some of the culturally disturbing ones, the Bible can be interpreted through the filter of liberation and social justice. One can also ask, in an effort to understand scripture, "How does this method help us interpret other biblical themes such as emancipation, deliverance, and justice for all people?"

To take this point of liberation further, we can explore the earthly ministry of Jesus. As I've stated before, it is important when studying a text to have an idea of the original intended audience. This allows us to find more in-depth meaning, with the hope of avoiding the distortion of scripture that can happen when looking at scripture out of its context. As an example, let's look at the beginning of Jesus's earthly ministry as it is recorded in the Gospel of Luke.

The community to which the author of Luke wrote was a body of believers living in the ancient Roman Empire. The Church has presumed that Luke, the physician and cohort of the Apostle Paul, was the author of this Gospel. His community was predominantly Gentile Christians with a minority Jewish Christian population.[7] Although the Jewish contingency may have been in the minority, scholars believe that there were some prominent and influential Jews in Luke's community, based on the culture and role of Jews in his account of the gospel.[8] Luke's account of the life and times of Jesus of Nazareth was probably written after 70 CE, using other previous written reports of Jesus as reference.[9] In his writing, Luke addresses a diverse group with various ethnic and economic backgrounds.[10]

It is clear, however, that Luke's account was written primarily for those on the lower end of the economic totem pole. In light of the huge gap between the wealthy and poor (not unlike today), it would seem inevitable that the poor would want some assurance and hope in the midst of their bondage to high taxation and mistreatment. The Roman government, with its structures that kept the rich wealthy and the poor impoverished, created an atmosphere of intimidation causing many of the lower class to acquiesce to their powerlessness.[11]

It is in the center of Roman domination and colonization that the Gospel of Luke was presented as a message of liberation for those on the fringes of society.[12] Jesus, as presented by Luke, was a breath of fresh air for the 99% of the population that struggled to survive in the elitist Roman Empire. Please keep in mind that Luke makes sense when we read it through the lens of hope and liberation.

Prior to the beginning of his earthly ministry, Luke 3:21-4:13 records that Jesus was baptized by his relative John, who was baptizing people in the wilderness and encouraging them to turn away from their sins. In the midst of Jesus's prayer, which took place during or shortly after his baptism, God said, "You are my Son, whom I dearly love; in you I find happiness" (Luke 3:22). Jesus, then endowed with the Holy Spirit, went into the wilderness and spent forty days fasting and overcoming the temptations of the devil. Notice that in this story Jesus knows what it is like to struggle, because here we see him tired and extremely hungry. The devil tries to manipulate and control Jesus. Yet Jesus is able to overcome. In other words, there was liberation. And how does Jesus overcome temptation? By quoting scripture. For Luke, liberation can come through studying and knowing scripture. It worked for Jesus. It can work for us too. This is where the Bible leads us, to the freedom of knowing God through the scripture and loving God and others as scripture commands.

V.

Helpful Tools

God does not want us to be ignorant. God wants to know us and for us to know God, because God loves us. So here are some tools that are embedded in the biblical text that can help us understand who God is, why we need God, and how we can know better what God expects from us and for us.

Some Key Biblical Principles

From the Old Testament to the New, there are key principles that you see running through the Bible's stories. The principles are present in the books of law, history, prophecy, and poetry, and certainly in the books and letters that describe the life and times of Jesus of Nazareth. One could argue that there are at least four major principles found throughout the Old and New Testaments. These principles are truths that serve as the basis of what we know about God. In other words, these concepts are what make Christianity what it is. The four principles are grace, mercy, the love of God, and forgiveness. While they are not always given these names, they are nevertheless very much present throughout the Bible.

Let's begin by defining these important concepts as simply as possible. There are several words that good Christians use and hear all the time. We sometimes use those words without having a clear understanding of what they mean. One reason why we don't have a clear understanding of some of the words we use is because they are closely related. The words "grace" and "mercy" are similar, but they are not the same. They are so close in meaning that we could call them twin sisters–they are related but not identical. Then there is God's love, which is also similar to grace and mercy but not the same. I would suggest to you that if grace and mercy are twin sisters then God's love is their mother. I'm going to do my best to try to distinguish between grace, mercy, and God's love.

Grace

Grace is God's unmerited love given to us that frees us from the power of sin. Grace is love that impacts us on an eternal level. Now in the Wesleyan branch of Christianity, grace is understood in phases or movements. There is prevenient grace. This refers to God's love that is present and available for us before we even recognize that there is a God. It is God's love that comes before our recognition. The Bible speaks of this kind of grace in 2 Timothy 1:8-10:

> So don't be ashamed of the testimony about the Lord or of me, his prisoner. Instead, share the suffering for the good news, depending on God's power. God is the one who saved and called us with a holy calling. This wasn't based on what we have done, but it was based on his own purpose and grace that he gave us in Christ Jesus before time began. Now his grace is revealed through the appearance of our savior, Christ Jesus. He destroyed death and brought life and immortality into clear focus through the good news.

Then once we recognize God's love and accept God's gracious gift of life through Christ Jesus, we move into justifying grace. Justifying grace represents the fact that we are pardoned and made right with God. We see an example of justifying grace in Romans 3:24-26.

> But all are treated as righteous freely by his grace because of a ransom that was paid by Christ Jesus. Through his faithfulness, God displayed Jesus as the place of sacrifice where mercy is found by means of his blood. He did this to demonstrate his righteousness in passing over sins that happened before, during the time of God's patient tolerance. He also did this to demonstrate that he is righteous in the present time, and to treat the one who has faith in Jesus as righteous.

The last movement of grace is sanctifying grace. This is God's love moving us toward holiness, that is, helping us to become more and more like Jesus–to love, talk, and act like Jesus. Ephesians 2:8-10 explains it this way:

> You are saved by God's grace because of your faith. This salvation is God's gift. It's not something you possessed. It's not something you did that you can be proud of. Instead, we are God's accomplishment, created in Christ Jesus to do good things. God planned for these good things to be the way that we live our lives.

Mercy

Grace is God's unmerited favor that leads to the salvation of our souls, while mercy is God's unmerited favor that rescues us from physical or emotional harm, danger, and oppression. Mercy has more to do with God's compassion. It is God's love expressed in the form of healing, deliverance, help, strength, comfort, and more. In short, grace and mercy are expressions of God's love. In that sense they are similar, and to be clear, a person cannot earn either one. Grace and mercy are given by God freely. But they differ in how they impact our lives. Not only does God show mercy to us but we too are to show mercy to one another.

God's Love

God's love is also freely given, but it is much broader than help from tangible danger and being rescued from the power of sin. God's love protects, restores, informs, instructs, plans, reconciles, sustains, guides, and directs our actions. It was out of love that God created everything in existence, especially humanity. Since God created us and loves us, it is God's intent to stay connected with us and get us back on track when we've gone astray. All of this is done out of love and for our benefit.

Great examples of the wide-ranging reach of God's love are found throughout the Old and New Testaments. In Romans 5 the Bible teaches that God's love builds us up to be stronger and more durable people. God's love authors hope in our lives because God is all about giving to us what we need when we need it.

The reason why God shows us grace, mercy, and love is because, as 1 John 4:7-9 says, God is love: "Dear friends, let's love each other, because love is from God, and everyone who loves is born from God and knows God. The person who doesn't love does not know God, because God is love. This is how the love of God is revealed to us: God has sent his only Son into the world so that we can live through him." But make no mistake. God is love, but love is not God. God is much more, and our notions of love cannot begin to describe all of who God is.

It is precisely because God is love that the love of God has always longed to rescue us, free us, and forgive us in order to become more than we thought possible. God cares and thinks about us and our well-being, even when we don't care about ourselves.

Forgiveness

Alongside the principles of grace, mercy, and God's love is the principle of forgiveness. This is something that is seen and experienced by people throughout the Bible. It is also foundational when it comes to understanding who God is and who we are as believers or even skeptics.

I've heard many people say that it seems like the Old and New Testaments are about different Gods. It appears that the God of the Old Testament is angry, vengeful, strict, and demanding. In short, the God we read about in the Old Testament seems impatient and not very forgiving. On the other hand, the God we read about in the New Testament seems nice, understanding, loving, and forgiving.

An example of a vengeful God is found in the Old Testament book of Jeremiah. The prophet Jeremiah relays a message to the people that comes from God. Remember, the Word of God was viewed as God speaking; it was not something written down. Jeremiah, in chapter four, tells the people of the Southern Kingdom of Judah that they would experience God's wrath, because of the evil they had committed. That is to say, God was fed up with the people and they would be punished as a result.

Many, however, would argue that God was merely acting like a loving parent who saw a child going astray and put the child in time-out to let them know the seriousness of their actions. Plus, punishment or discipline is a way of steering people back onto the right path. Nevertheless, the mere notion that God punishes people leads many to view God as scary.

In contrast, the descriptions of God in the New Testament are that of a loving and forgiving God. An example of this is found in Romans 8:38-39. The Apostle Paul explains that there is absolutely nothing that will prevent God from loving us through Christ Jesus. The thought of God loving us unconditionally is encouraging and comforting. It is one of the most powerful passages of scripture and helps us understand that God is loving and forgiving.

So why does there seem to be such a difference between God in the Old Testament and God in the New Testament? It has led some to read the New Testament only and avoid the Old Testament altogether. However, I would argue that the Old Testament shows a very loving and forgiving God just as we see in the New Testament. But the way to really get that understanding of God in the first testament is to understand the context of time. There is a huge difference in the time frame of the two testaments. The period of time from the age of Abraham that we read about in the book of Genesis to the birth of Jesus that we read about in the New Testament books of Matthew and Luke is over 3,000 years. On the other hand, the New Testament, from the birth of Jesus to the period of the apostles and the writing of the Gospels, is roughly 70 to 80 years. That is a huge difference in time.

Why does that matter? It is easy to read something like the book of Jeremiah and believe that God is vengeful and unforgiving. After all, God punished the people, some might say harshly, because they made mistakes and turned away from God to worship other gods. But when you read the Old Testament with the understanding of the time period it covers, it makes more sense. Without that understanding of time, we don't realize that God put up with that disobedient behavior for a long time before there was any type of punishment. In the Old Testament book of Nehemiah chapter

9 we learn there were generations of rebelliousness from the people without any retribution. But at some point, God, just like any parent, has to respond in some form or fashion to disobedience. Because of this, Nehemiah chapter 9 also declares that God is slow to anger. After all, God let things slide for generations. Not only is God slow to anger, but Nehemiah says God is also forgiving. It took years before God's anger spilled over into what the Bible identifies as wrath, God's righteous anger.

The second thing to understand about God being forgiving even in the writings of the Old Testament is that the people's understanding of God evolved over time. And I would hope that our understanding of God continues to evolve. At one point, people believed that everything came from God: the good, the bad, the ugly, and the weird. In the stories of 1 Samuel and Exodus we read about God sending an evil spirit to someone. In Samuel it was Israel's first king, Saul, and in Exodus it was the pharaoh of Egypt. For modern-day readers that seems strange, but in ancient times that's how they understood things to work. Keep in mind, they also thought the world was flat and if a couple couldn't have a child, it was solely the woman's fault. We know those things to be untrue today.

As I mentioned, ancient people believed that everything, even bad happenings, comes from God, and in a sense it does since God created everything. However, today we might explain things more as cause and effect. That is to say, the people of God came to know and accept that we are reaping the consequences of our own actions. Moreover, we understand that some of the bad things that happen to us (ancient people would view it as punishment) are a result of circumstance. Jesus explains about bad things happening to good people and good things happening to bad people in

Matthew 5:45: "your Father who is in heaven . . . makes the sun rise on both the evil and the good and sends rain on both the righteous and the unrighteous." And the Old Testament story of Job teaches that bad things happen to good and bad people just like good things happen to bad and good people alike. The difference between many people today and people of ancient times is that when something went wrong in the lives of ancient people, their explanation was that they must have done something to offend God. That's how they made sense of the world and life.

It's important to reiterate that we know more today about so many things than people did thousands of years ago. Just like humanity as a whole has evolved in knowledge, so too have believers in terms of how we understand and relate to God. But our knowledge, understanding, and appreciation for God is built upon the foundation of what was passed down from previous generations, including and perhaps especially the biblical writers.

I think what is also worth mentioning to modern readers of scripture is that the people of the Old Testament would have probably been shocked to hear people say that God was vengeful and unforgiving. That wasn't their understanding at all. The poetic and wisdom book of Psalms is full of expressions of how loving and forgiving God is. There are psalms that talk about how good God is, there is no one like God, and God is faithful through all generations.

The last thing I want to say about understanding the forgiveness of God, even in the Old Testament, is that people of that time believed God cared for them and wanted them to do well even when they were disobedient. When you read the prophetic writings from Isaiah to Malachi, you see God's punishment of the people because of their waywardness; but there is something else you will read. God seems to always have a plan to bring the people out of their punishment and liberate them. The punishment is only for a season and for a purpose, and once it is over God promises to restore the people to their previous fortunes and sometimes to even greater heights. Some might refer to this as God's tough love, and the key word is love. But the fact that God also promises to restore the people puts God's love and forgiveness on full display in the Old Testament.

God's plan is always to restore us.

What does all of this say for us today? First, it lets us know that God is patient. God is not some dictator who sits high above us waiting to zap anyone who does anything that contradicts what God requires. God gives us chance after chance, because God knows we are infinitely flawed and lack knowledge and sometimes willpower.

Second, God loves us so much that words really can't explain it completely. Because God created us, God has a vested interest in us that moves God to stick with us and never give up on us. That vested interest, simply put, is love.

Most of all, God's plans are always to restore us. In fact, most of the Bible is filled with stories of God working to restore humanity in one way or another. The purpose of the great flood in the book of Genesis, the story of Noah and his family surviving, is all about God starting over in an effort to restore humanity back to its intended greatness–the greatness that was stained and broken in the Garden of Eden when humanity disobeyed God. The reason why God made a covenant with Abraham was so that humanity could be restored. The hope was that through this covenant all the earth would be brought into good standing with God. The reason God gave Moses commandments was so that the people would have rules that would help guide them to a state of restoration from the destruction that was caused by lawlessness. Finally, Jesus died on the cross because God wanted to restore humanity from its fall and constant sin. It is through that act of Jesus that all people have access to complete forgiveness by God.

Idolatry and the Mistreatment of the Poor

The opposite of living with grace, mercy, love, and forgiveness is worshipping something or someone more than God–idolatry–and mistreating the poor. The law books of the Bible give us ten commandments and over 600 statutes. All of these rules were to be followed, but there seemed to be some that caused the people of God more problems, as a whole, than any others. The prophetic books are full of oracles declaring that God was going to respond to generations of disobedience, and it really boiled down to a couple of things. The two biggest reasons people in biblical times needed forgiveness and perhaps why we need it so much today are idolatry and mistreating the poor.

What may seem strange to modern readers of the Bible is that for much of the Old Testament the writers did not deny that other gods existed. Of course, as time went on there was the declaration that there is no god except the Lord. But initially people believed that there were multiple gods. What distinguished the descendants of Abraham from other people was that they followed only one God. In fact, when God gave Moses the Ten Commandments, God didn't say, "Don't waste your time with any other gods than me because there are no other gods." Exodus 34:14 could be understood to say quite the opposite: "You must not bow down to another god, because the LORD is passionate: the

LORD's name means 'a passionate God.'" That is to say that God is jealous and requires complete faithfulness.

Other nations worshipped various gods for various things. There was a god of war, a god of fertility, a god of the moon, a god of the sun, a god of water, and so on. While these other nations had many gods to appease, Israel was to honor only one. But it was their constant acceptance of gods from other nations for generations that brought about God's righteous indignation. This was not something that happened every now and then, it was sort of habitual. Instead of influencing other peoples to follow their God, the one true God, they would adopt these false deities as their own. This invariably led to punishment (correction), but God, being loving, would forgive them and ultimately restore them.

Let me say that the same thing happens with us today. Although we might not worship statues of gods, we do devote our time, energy, and even money to material things that take our attention away from God. Yet God is still willing to forgive us as well. When the people persisted in disobeying and worshipping other gods, there were penalties. We see this played out in 2 Kings 17, more specifically in verses 7-8,

> All this happened because the Israelites sinned against the LORD their God, who brought them up from the land of Egypt, out from under the power of Pharaoh, Egypt's king. They worshipped other gods. They followed the practices of the nations that the LORD had removed before the Israelites, as well as the practices that the Israelite kings had done.

The other law that was broken consistently was not taking care of the poor. The poor in ancient society were made up of, for the most part, widows, orphans, and foreigners/strangers. There are countless verses that recount God's demand to look after those who need help. One such passage is found in Deuteronomy 14:28-29,

> Every third year you must bring the tenth part of your produce from that year and leave it at your city gates. Then the Levites, who have no designated inheritance like you do, along with the immigrants, orphans, and widows who live in your cities, will come and feast until they are full. Do this so that the LORD your God might bless you in everything you do.

If the Bible is clear on anything, it is that God requires the faithful to protect and help those on the margins of society.

Unfortunately, the ancient Israelites fell into the same practices as other societies from antiquity and modern times in that the poor were continually neglected. As a result of such disobedience, there were consequences. Widows were poor because, in that time and in that society, women were often completely provided for by their fathers and then husbands. Once the husband was dead, women would have been left to the mercy, or lack thereof, of society. Of course, children without parents, or really without a father, to provide for them would have been reduced to homeless beggars, as they did not have systems in place like we do today to care for them.

Strangers/foreigners would have been in a similar category, but there was more to it than meets the eye. Coming from a different land with different customs, they would have stuck out. It would have been easy for the natural citizens to ignore them. But more importantly, because they were not part of the twelve tribes of Israel, they would not have the same property rights. They would have entered the land of Israel already at a disadvantage. Moreover, because of Israel's own history of being strangers in a distant land

(Egypt) they were charged to be more sympathetic to others. Exodus 22:21 says, "Don't mistreat or oppress an immigrant, because you were once immigrants in the land of Egypt." Basically God was saying, "You know what it feels like to be mistreated, but because you are different, you ought to know better."

In spite of the fact of being warned about taking advantage of those who were downtrodden, the people ignored the poor's plight. Regrettably the exploitation of the underprivileged still takes place today. For the people in biblical times this mistreatment meant that, at some point, they would have to reap the consequences of those actions or inactions. Zechariah 7:8-14 explains this perfectly,

> The LORD's word came to Zechariah:
>
> The LORD of heavenly forces proclaims:
>
> Make just and faithful decisions; show kindness and compassion to each other! Don't oppress the widow, the orphan, the stranger, and the poor; don't plan evil against each other! But they refused to pay attention. They turned a cold shoulder and stopped listening.
>
> They steeled their hearts against hearing the Instruction and the words that the LORD of heavenly forces sent by his spirit through the earlier prophets. As a result, the LORD of heavenly forces became enraged.
>
> So just as he called and they didn't listen, when they called, I didn't listen, says the LORD of heavenly forces. I scattered them throughout the nations whom they didn't know. The land was devastated behind them, with no one leaving or returning. They turned a delightful land into a wasteland.

It seems clear that one of the things that is extremely important to God is care for poor and unfortunate individuals and groups. Therefore, when trying to make sense of the Bible, it stands to reason that using God's care for the poor to help provide light on some seemingly obscure passages of scripture is a helpful guide.

Scripture within Scripture

Another tool to understand the Bible is using those passages that encapsulate the big story of God that the Bible tells. There are certain passages of scripture that capture the ethos of the Bible as a whole. That is to say, they incarnate the key principles and summarize what the Bible is all about. Because these verses embody the spirit of the Bible, they can be used to interpret and understand other scripture. They are especially useful when reading some of those more troubling and challenging passages that we talked about earlier, and there are plenty.

John 3:16

There are two scriptures in particular that I believe personify the hope, spirit, and even purpose of the Bible. They have become sacred verses in and of themselves. The first is John 3:16, "God so loved the world that he gave his only Son, so that everyone who believes in him won't perish but will have eternal life." This verse has become so popular that you can see fans holding it up on signs at sporting events. I would dare to say that even people not familiar with church or the Bible know this verse.

The reason this scripture is so important is because it gives us a real glimpse into who God is and how God operates. This one verse has so much meaning that I could preach it a hundred different times and a hundred different ways.

The scripture begins with love, the love that God has for every human being. That love God shows to the world is given without any human asking for or even thinking about it. In fact, there is no indication that the world even deserves God's love, yet God still loves the world. To bring the point home even more it says "God so loved." That "so" indicates that God's love is, as the children's song says, "deep and wide." God loved the world so much, in spite of our disobedience and cluelessness, that God gave Jesus to the world. The love is expressed in the gift of salvation that God gives to the world. This means that everyone has access to life eternal as a result of God's unmerited love–God's grace. The fact that it says God loved the world means everyone is included in it.

Romans 5:8

The other passage that I view as scripture within scripture is Romans 5:8, "But God shows his love for us, because while we were still sinners Christ died for us." The reason why God first spoke to humanity was out of love. Even though humanity was not living up and has not lived up to God's expectations, God never stops loving us; after all, God created us. It is out of that love that God spoke to priests, prophets, kings, and others so that we would know how to be in relationship with God and each other. What God spoke was eventually written down in what we now call the Bible. Furthermore, it was out of love that God's Word became a living and breathing organism–Jesus–who offered himself as a sacrifice so all might be reconnected with our creator. That is evidence of God's love for us, and it is at the core of why God spoke and speaks to us through scripture and through a variety of other means.

These two passages of scripture are similar in that both emphasize that God is the one who initiates love toward us regardless of who we are and where we are in life. It does not matter what you've done; God loves you. It does not matter if you don't even love yourself; God still loves you. It does not matter if you don't think you are worthy of anyone's love; God believes that you are. These two verses provide us a context for understanding other scripture.

While we may have questions about some of the things that we read in the Bible, if we refer to scripture within scripture along with the themes and principles of scripture, we can gain a greater appreciation for what we read, even some of the challenging texts.

Scripture is, for most religions, the foundation for all that is believed. Christians call these collected writings the Bible. It lays the foundation for what we believe as followers of Jesus. Every book and every verse in the Bible is important; however, there are some verses that stand out and have more impact and meaning than others. It's not that these passages are more sacred than others, but they capture the essence of what scripture is all about. Therefore, these particular texts can be used as tools to help connect us to what God's intent is for us as we study the scriptures.

It's sort of like the movie *The Sixth Sense*, which is about a boy who is able to see the ghosts of dead people. He is helped by a child psychologist who we find out at the end of the movie is actually dead himself. For the entire movie, it is the ghost of the child psychologist that counsels the young boy, and the audience has no idea until the end. Once you know that the psychologist has been dead all along, it does two things. First, it gives a new perspective on the entire film. To me, what made the movie so good was that the psychologist was dead for most of the movie and we didn't know it. I thought I understood the movie perfectly and then when the bombshell hit at the end, it added new meaning. Secondly, it helps to make greater sense of some of the earlier scenes. We can reflect back on what we saw earlier, and it adds more value to the film. That's precisely what these certain texts do for the Bible. They help give us a new perspective, and they help us make sense of some of the other things in scripture that don't seem to register right away in our minds.

These two texts, John 3:16 and Romans 5:8, are only meant to be representative. There are others, but once you have a grasp of these and texts like them, you get a better sense of God's intent for the world. To put it another way, these passages help lay the groundwork for everything else we read about what God is doing in the rest of scripture.

I think it is also helpful to view the Bible as more than just a literary piece of work. It is helpful to see scripture as conveying a living, breathing organism–the Holy Spirit–that is meant to give guidance, direction, and purpose to those who read it. It's not that every single word in the story is an exact blueprint of how we should live. It is more as if the scriptures are saying, "Look at my life, the good, the bad, and the ugly. Learn from it and adapt it to your modern context."

Loving Like Jesus

Another tool is to look to the words and follow the actions of Jesus as found in the New Testament Gospel books: Matthew, Mark, Luke, and John. They will illuminate other parts of the Bible. When one is trying to make sense of something in the Bible, paying special attention to the wisdom and compassion of Jesus's words can clarify things. Matthew 5:17 says, "Don't even begin to think that I have come to do away with the Law and the Prophets. I haven't come to do away with them but to fulfill them." If Jesus is the embodiment of the law of Moses and the one about whom the prophets prophesied, then it seems only right to use his life and teachings as a tool to bring life to the rest of scripture. After all, he is the focal point.

The acts and words of Jesus embody the principles that we looked at earlier. Jesus personifies God's love, grace, mercy, and forgiveness. The truth of the matter is that the life and teachings of Jesus summarize God's intent for the world. Whenever I come across a scripture that seems to be a bit cruel and just the opposite of who we know God to be, I do several things. First, I try to understand the historical context. Second, I hold the scripture up to the light of God's love, mercy, and grace. Third, I remind myself that whatever the scripture says, God is a God of liberation and justice. Last, I read scripture through the lens of the words of Jesus.

The Bible Is Not All Facts, but It Is All Truth

If you did a thorough historical examination of the Bible you would quickly discover there are historical inaccuracies. There are names, places, and times in scripture that simply contradict what we know to be historically correct. The biblical authors weren't concerned as much with exact and precise chronology, places, and people as they were with the underlying message of the story. This is why there is some non-factual content in the Bible, but the truth is still there.

The book of Genesis shares stories of people living to be hundreds of years old, such as Noah, who the Bible says lived to be over 900. We know that a person living 900 years is factually impossible from our modern vantage point; I will also say that with God all things are possible. The point of sharing that Noah was that old is to suggest to the reader that he lived a long time, which for ancient peoples was a sign of God's blessing. The truth is he lived many years and was favored by God. Whether he lived 900 years is not the point.

Exodus 38:26 says: "They gave a beqa per person (that is, half a shekel, measured by the sanctuary shekel) for everyone who was counted in the census, 20 years old and above, 603,550 men." If there were over 600,000 men, this would mean that over 1 million people were led out of Egypt by Moses, because that number does not include women and children. Factually it would be impossible for that many people to wander about together in the desert terrain. In fact, it would be a miracle, which is the point. And Egyptian records do not mention any exodus that large. Most likely, the truth of the story is that a relatively large group of Hebrews (large in the minds of the Hebrews) left Egypt on their way to a Promised Land.

Another story that is probably not 100 percent factual is found in the second chapter of the Gospel of Matthew. In this story it says that King Herod had all the boys two years and under around Bethlehem slaughtered. Many scholars have argued that it did not really happen or at least not as Matthew implies. While Herod may or may not have had dozens of boys killed, the story is meant to show how ruthless and paranoid he was as a ruler. That is the truth of the story, while the facts continue to be heavily disputed. As I've stated already, the biblical writers used hyperbole to make a point designed to help readers see a bigger picture with the hope that the reader would focus on God's truth rather than details of a story.

Although the Bible is not completely factual, it is all truth. That is to say some of that data may not be precise, but the intent and purpose is to convey truth, the truth being that which is dependable and durable, because it has been tried and tested. The truth is that the Bible contains the knowledge and wisdom of the ages that has produced the ethical and moral foundation for most of the Western world and people all over the globe. The narrative of scripture provides principled lessons that transcend culture and generations. If you look beyond the customs of the ancient people and focus on the lessons, you can find meaning and purpose for our current realities.

The Bible contains wisdom and truth.

Please know that I'm not suggesting everything we read in the Bible is fictional, because many of the stories have actually been validated with sources outside of scripture, including archaeology. However, I believe the truth is more valuable than fact, because fact only provides you with information, but truth gives you a firm foundation for living. Remember the Bible is not a history or science book, it is God's story.

VI.

So What?

Jesus's Life, Ministry, and Resurrection

One could argue, and rightfully so, that the summation of the Bible can be found in the life, teachings, death, and, most of all, the resurrection of Jesus of Nazareth. Jesus was a peripatetic–itinerant–teacher who went from village to village in the Galilean and Judean regions of first-century Palestine. He shared a message about the Kingdom of God with the intent of ushering in a new era of love, justice, and freedom for all people.

One of the reasons why the Bible is relevant is because, in Jesus, it shows us the perfect example of how we are to live. He was (*is*, because he still lives) a walking and breathing illustration of compassion for the hurting and justice for the marginalized, and he was a bridge-builder for people with differences. From his life we can even learn how to forgive people who have misused and abused us.

The Bible is also important because it contains information about God's kingdom, God's intent for us and the world, and God's preferred future. It gives us stories of what it is like. And through Jesus we get a glimpse of what our God-given role is in creating a kingdom atmosphere on earth that is similar to the one in heaven.

We find Jesus's own summary of his ministry in Luke 4:18-19: "The Spirit of the Lord is upon me, because the Lord has anointed me. He has sent me to preach good news to the poor, to proclaim release to the prisoners and recovery of sight to the blind, to liberate the oppressed, and to proclaim the year of the Lord's favor." This is what Jesus was born to do. Because it is Jesus's mission, it is also the mandate of all who follow him. It also suggests how we ought to view the Bible in light of this mission and mandate. Jesus, being led by the Holy Spirit, enters the synagogue, a place where people gathered for study and worship, in his hometown of Nazareth. It is important to note that Nazareth was a poor village, and consequently people considered it unimportant. It was such a small "backwoods" place that someone once uttered, "Can anything from Nazareth be good?" (John 1:46).

The fact that Jesus is from Nazareth is meant to let the reader know that God is with those who live in desolate places, whether the desolation is physical, psychological, social, or emotional. All of this happens right after Jesus spent forty days fasting and being tempted in the wilderness.

Jesus uses the scroll of Isaiah as a point of departure for announcing his public ministry to his hometown. Using Isaiah gives Jesus credibility for his ministry, because he establishes his mission on the authority of scripture.[13]

Jesus's proclamation, as recorded in Luke, comes from a combination of texts from Isaiah, namely, chapters 61 and 58. The Spirit of the Lord has commissioned Jesus and all those who follow him for a specific assignment. That assignment is to liberate those who are oppressed. The fact that it does not name explicit types of oppression means that it is not limited. That is to say, whatever systems and structures place roadblocks in people's lives, Jesus is against them. He came to do away with those structures, so that those who are bound by them can be free to live a full life. This passage lets us know that Jesus's ministry involves releasing people from all types of physical, social, and emotional subjugation. Luke clearly implies that Jesus was sent to restore those on the margins of the society to a place of acceptance and wholeness.

In this passage from Luke, we see Jesus quote from Isaiah 61, which connects with the proclamation of the year of Jubilee. Leviticus 25 required that every fiftieth year be a year of freedom and reconciliation. The Jubilee laws required that no crops were to be sown, all debts were to be cancelled, and any Israelite in slavery was to be set free. It was also a time when the land, which had originally been given by God according to ancestral lines, was to be returned to the descendants of the original recipients. The Jubilee year was a time when things were to be set back in order, giving the poor an opportunity to have the freedom and wholeness God intended. By referencing the Jubilee, this account makes clear that Jesus's ministry was to serve the purpose of helping those who were ignored and despised by the larger society.

After Jesus finished with the scroll of Isaiah, he stated his purpose for being there. In verse 20 we see that everyone in the synagogue was waiting in great anticipation to see what Jesus had to say about the scripture. I can imagine that Jesus knew how to get the people's attention and took his time before speaking in order to create a dramatic pause. As all eyes were fixed on him, we can imagine what the people were thinking. After years of waiting on God's promise of a messiah, a savior, finally, he had come. And the initial response that Jesus received was positive. The town's people who were gathered in the synagogue were astonished at his teachings and spoke highly of Jesus, even if some had concerns surrounding his familial origin.

The Nazarenes–and we must imagine there were members of Jesus's family and extended family there–were shocked to hear Jesus, the son of Joseph the carpenter, speak like a prophet. Jesus told them he was sure they would want him to perform miracles in his hometown as he had done in Capernaum, a town not too far away. But Jesus did not perform miracles; instead he told them how a prophet is generally not accepted in his place of birth, by those who watched him grow up. Jesus even cited examples of other prophets who were rejected by their own, performed miracles, and cured hated foreigners–from leprosy, the worst of diseases. When Jesus's hometown neighbors heard this and thought about the implication of Jesus's words, they were so livid that they drove Jesus out of town to the crest of the hill upon which the town was constructed, intending to throw him off and kill him. Yet miraculously Jesus was able to walk directly through the angry mob and went on his way.

What can we glean from this dramatic story? For the original intended readers, it was surely to give hope in the midst of oppression. This passage gives assurance to those on the margins of an elitist society that they too can have deliverance from dreary circumstances. It encourages the followers of Jesus to keep the faith in the one who can set them free from their sins and from their social, political, and economic shackles. When the original readers of this text read about justice, they knew that through Jesus they had access to power coupled with an expectation that even in the face of opposition, they could experience the freedom of the Jubilee, the "year of the Lord's favor."

What interests me about this text, as it relates to how we ought to read and understand scripture, is that it is about release from all types of restraints and it gives us the means by which we can make sense of scripture in any age. If Jesus's entire ministry was rooted in liberation–setting people free–then it makes sense to use that as a lens to help us understand what scripture means for us today.

Putting What You Read into Practice

Putting what you read into practice is connected with faith. It is through faith that one has a desire to live the principles and teachings found in the Bible. The word "faith" is usually associated with something that a person has within themselves as a sort of a possession. In my experience, many believers explain faith as a mindset. According to these believers, faith means having a deep trust in God. While I agree with that definition, I believe it is the first part of a twofold meaning of faith. It is my contention that faith can also be defined in terms of one's actions. Faith is not only a deep trust and belief in God, but it also entails the way one acts out that trust and belief on a daily basis.

Keep in mind what I shared earlier: it is by way of faith that people receive God's Word through scripture, dreams, in whatever form. God's Word, found in scripture, only has value if we use it to impact our life. It is faith that pushes us and entices us to read the Bible. It is faith that helps us to understand the Bible in the context of our lives.

"Faith" is a word that isn't always explained easily, because it has many implications and components that make up its complex meaning. It is faith that directs our actions and shapes how we look at the world. For people who strive to follow Jesus, faith is directed toward God's action in Jesus on the cross and in resurrection. Because Christian faith is focused on Jesus, what we read about him must become part of the foundation of how we read the Bible in the first place. The resurrection is the highlight of the Christian Bible, and even before we had what we now call the Bible, it was news of the resurrection that believers passed down by word of mouth from one generation to the next.

Before people got the full story of Jesus's birth, life, and teachings they received word of his resurrection from the grave. The truth of the matter is that the resurrection is the single most important event in the Christian tradition. It is very well likely that without the resurrection of Jesus, we would not have a religion called Christianity. And the true message of the resurrection of Jesus is that, as Jeff Goldblum's character stated in the movie *Jurassic Park*, "life finds a way." To say it another way, those who have life through Jesus can conquer all obstacles, including death. Furthermore, having faith in the power of the resurrection enables us to live life with a strong sense of victory.

Reading the Bible for Personal Meaning

There are different ways to approach the question of the Bible's meaning in a specific passage of scripture. The reason is that each passage can be packed with meaning, and as I've laid out earlier in this book, there are a number of ways of interpreting them. But more important is how we find meaning for our personal lives from the Bible.

The meaning of a certain text can be discovered, in some sense, by studying the historical context–that is to say, what was going on culturally during the time in which the text was written. That helps you answer the question of what it meant for the original intended readers. That meaning may speak to your circumstances, but again you might need to search deeper. You may need to take the meaning of a text that was intended for the original readers and adapt it to modern times. So ask yourself, "What is the spirit of the scripture for me in the here and now?"

Here is an example. Matthew 22:21 says, "Then he [Jesus] said, 'Give to Caesar what belongs to Caesar and to God what belongs to God.'" Here Jesus explains that you should not deny God in order to fulfill your other obligations, and vice versa. For the people living in the day of Jesus, this was easy to understand. "Caesar" was the title used by Roman emperors, and Jesus lived in the Roman Empire. Once you understand that, then you know Jesus was suggesting that one should pay what is owed to the government, and this should not interfere with what you are to give God. This text might seem self-explanatory, but if someone ignores the historical context, they could look for someone named Caesar to give money to because Jesus said so. That is a literal interpretation. Or you could say, "Since the government I live under is not Caesar, I don't have to give anything." This is rudimentary, to be sure, but I'm simply trying to make the point that for a text to have real meaning for modern readers, you have to adapt it from its original context. When you do, it makes perfect sense that Jesus was merely saying to give taxes to the government as it is required and give to God what is required, which is yourself.

Even if one adapts the original meaning, the text may not have much value for you in your personal life at the time, and that is okay. Sometimes different passages have different value for us at different periods of our lives depending on where we are. You could make the argument that there is the original meaning, the modern contextual meaning, and what the text says to me in my personal life. What a text means for you personally may not apply to others, and more than likely it will not. In order for you to find personal meaning, you will need to evaluate your individual context. What's going on with you emotionally, socially, physically, relationally, and psychologically? Evaluating where you are will open you up to how a particular text relates to your circumstance.

Most Christians believe that all scripture is inspired by God, and I would add that it is Spirit-filled, meaning, the Holy Spirit is constantly working in and through the words, stories, and pages of the Bible to accomplish God's purposes in us. That being the case, a great way to find value that addresses you personally is to ask God to reveal it to you. Pray about it. Then as you read, ask God to speak to you and your situation through the text. It's in this approach that you find what the Bible means for you. This is not an academic exercise but a faith-forming practice where you discover what God is saying to you individually.

If We Have the Bible, Do We Still Need the Church?

Some might argue that if we have the Bible, we might not really need preachers or even need the Church. Others would make the point that in order to truly live out what the Bible teaches, it is critical that one belong to a local faith community, a church of Jesus Christ. I want to shed a little light on this subject by answering these questions: Do you have to belong to a church to be part of God's people, and why is belonging to a congregation helpful?

There are a great many people who, when they hear the word "Christian," make the connection with going to a house of worship on Sunday. Of course this concept was uprooted when the coronavirus hit and people were unable to gather in a building for worship. But aside from pandemics, this viewpoint maintains that if you are a Christian, you are supposed to go to a church. And I do want to emphasize that the Bible never refers to a building as a church; a church is a gathering of believers. But for many, being a Christian means you are a member of a local congregation and you participate regularly. But is that necessarily the case? Let's look at this more closely. A Christian in the simplest definition is one who follows the teachings and examples of Jesus the Christ.

To take that a step further one might make reference to Romans 10:9, which states, "Because if you confess with your mouth 'Jesus is Lord' and in your heart you have faith that God raised him from the dead, you will be saved." We could go into more detail but this is the abbreviated version of what it means to be a Christian. The word we get for "church" comes from the Greek *ekklesia*, which means a gathering of people called out from their homes. It was a gathering of people coming together for one purpose. Not long after Jesus ascended into heaven, believers began using the term to refer to people who congregated together in the name of the Lord. The word for "church" is used 115 times in the New Testament, many of them in Acts.

The word for "church" is used in at least three ways in the New Testament. Acts 14:27-28 says, "On their arrival, they gathered the church together and reported everything that God had accomplished through their activity, and how God had opened a door of faith for the Gentiles. They stayed with the disciples a long time." This passage makes reference to a local congregation in a specific city. This is what is most commonly called a church today: a community of people who worship and do ministry together. While the concept of denominations was foreign to the first century, there were, nevertheless, different faith groups. In this sense, a local congregation is only a representative of the total body of believers.

Another way the word is used is found in Colossians 1:24-25: "Now I'm happy to be suffering for you. I'm completing what is missing from Christ's sufferings with my own body. I'm doing this for the sake of his body, which is the church. I became a servant of the church by God's commission, which was given to me for you, in order to complete God's word." In this sense the word for "church" refers to the catholic Church. Not catholic as in Roman Catholic but as in the universal Church. The Church is made up of every person who claims Jesus regardless of their local congregation or denomination. The Church is made up of every believer, which today is around 2 billion worldwide. All believers make up the body of Christ in the world today. That means that Jesus is still tangibly engaged in the world right now. We live out what we learn from the Bible by serving as the eyes, the ears, the voice, the hands, the heart, and the feet of Jesus on the earth right now.

The other way the word "church" is used is in reference to the community of believers who await the final consummation of our relationship with Jesus. In Ephesians 5:29-32 we learn that there will be a marriage between Jesus and his Church. "No one ever hates his own body, but feeds it and takes care of it just like Christ does for the church because we are parts of his body. *This is why a man will leave his father and mother and be united with his wife, and the two of them will be one body.* Marriage is a significant allegory, and I'm applying it to Christ and the church." We as individuals love our spouses. This passage suggests that the relationship between Jesus and the Church is loving, giving, intimate, and sacrificial.

Revelation 19:7 says: "Let us rejoice and celebrate, and give him the glory, for the wedding day of the Lamb has come, and his bride has made herself ready." Here again we see the connection that is made between earthly marriage and Jesus's relationship with believers. We learn that eventually Jesus will become one with us in mission and ministry, in purpose and intent for the good of all creation. That will be the completion or the fulfillment of the work and ministry of the Church on earth and the ushering in of God's Kingdom. This will be the day when Jesus returns and all our unhealthy divisions will be overcome.

Having said all that, I would argue that you don't have to go to a church as much as you have to be part of the Church to truly be a follower of Jesus. However, I would argue that in order to grow as a follower of Jesus, being a part of a local congregation is vital. God created us to live out our faith not in isolation but in community.

How Church Helps Us Live Our Faith

First I want to establish why the Church is important in the first place. In Matthew 16:18 Jesus declares, "I tell you that you are Peter. And I'll build my church on this rock. The gates of the underworld won't be able to stand against it." Jesus makes this statement during a conversation he has with his followers. He wants to know who people say that he is. His disciples respond by saying that some people think he is one of the prophets or even John the Baptist. Jesus cuts them off and wants to know what they think. I envision that there was silence; and then Peter, always being the bold one, shouts out that he is the messiah–the son of the God of the universe. Jesus tells him that he is correct, knowing that Peter didn't come up with that on his own, but that it was revealed to him by God. Remember, there are some things humans cannot know unless it is revealed to us. Jesus then states that it is upon the type of faith that Peter has shown that the Church will be built.

It doesn't matter how long you have been a member of a congregation; it's not your church. It doesn't matter if you are the pastor or a prominent leader; it is not your church. The Church and every congregation belong to Jesus. And the reason why the Church is important is because Jesus founded it. Jesus gave his life for it. Jesus's intent is that the Church acts on his behalf until he returns in glory. I don't believe that Jesus would establish something that was meant to be ignored. The very fact that Jesus established the Church suggests that it must be important.

I want to propose that there are at least four reasons why you ought to belong to a local church. They are all critical when it comes to putting faith into practice. Those reasons are accountability, encouragement, understanding, and growth. We should not overlook the fact that scripture warns us not to ignore the value of consistently gathering together with other believers. It states in Hebrews 10:25, "Don't stop meeting together with other believers, which some people have gotten into the habit of doing. Instead, encourage each other, especially as you see the day drawing near."

Accountability

Everyone needs to be held accountable–otherwise it is hard to live up to God's standards. It is hard to be your best in isolation. Now we all fall short anyway, but we can lose our moral compass when we aren't surrounded by others who are striving for the same things. Having small groups, Sunday school classes, and prayer partners helps us stay on track and live lives worthy of calling ourselves disciples of Jesus. This is why in the early days of the Methodist movement in the British Isles and the US, Wesley and his followers established classes or small groups to help one another to maintain a morally excellent lifestyle.

Encouragement

Another reason why being a part of a church is important is the opportunity to receive and give encouragement during times of challenge. Regardless of how strong one is emotionally, there are some things a person simply cannot handle alone. When you are suffering from grief, it's easier to deal with if you have others who are with you to give support with their prayers and presence. Church communities are centers for providing emotional support and care because as disciples of Jesus this is what we've been called to do.

I remember several years ago when Kansas City had an ice storm I saw something that made it clear to me the importance of having a church home. There were tree branches on the ground all over the city. They simply snapped because of the weight of the ice. However, I noticed a group of trees that were in close proximity to one another. The branches on those trees had ice on them as well, yet they were bent and not broken. The reason was that the branches were leaning against branches from the other trees. The branches from the trees supported one another during a time of challenge. Although you may bend during times of trials, difficulty, and sorrow, the Church of Jesus Christ through local congregations is designed to keep you from breaking.

Being part of a local church is important for faith development because it helps us understand the Bible better. Of course you can read and study on your own, but I believe that will only take you so far. When you are able to study the Bible with others, whether in a classroom or small-group setting, it can only enhance your perspective. Others are able to see some things that you might not recognize because we all come with our own unique background and perspective.

Understanding

I remember my family and I went to see a movie. Afterwards we talked about it. While we all agreed what the movie was truly about, we each had a unique take on it. All of us offered something that the others had not noticed, thought about, or considered. Had we not talked about it, all of us would have had only our individual perspective on the movie. But because of our conversation, we were able to help each other appreciate the movie even more. This is the reason why high school and college students develop study groups. They recognize they have a much better chance of understanding class material working together than they do isolated from each other. The same is true when studying the Bible with others who are connected with a church.

Proverbs 27:17 says, "As iron sharpens iron, so one person sharpens a friend." In other words, we become stronger as individuals when we connect with others who are trying to become stronger. When you have a group of individuals connected to and believing in the same God, it means you have common purpose. You are all moving in the same direction. The bottom line is that having a church home helps you to grow in your walk with the Lord. Spending time with others on the same journey as you is inspirational and helpful because you're building each other up.

Growth

The fourth reason having a church home is important is because it helps you to develop in the same way going to a health club to exercise helps you become stronger. I've heard a number of people say that you are more likely to exercise if you have someone to exercise with you. Because you have someone encouraging and pushing you, it is more likely you will continue to move toward your health goals and eventually achieve them.

Your spiritual growth works the same way. When you have others who encourage and lovingly push you to grow spiritually, you are more likely to continue moving toward your goal. Associating with others with similar interests is a form of spiritual exercise. This is often referred to as Christian fellowship. Praying and worshipping with others along with fellowship are means to help us become stronger in the Lord, making them great reasons to stay connected to a community of faith.

To grow in faith and live out biblical principles, having a church home is beyond helpful, it is necessary. Acts 2:42-47 summarizes it best. Here we read that "the believers devoted themselves to the apostles' teaching, to the community, to their shared meals, and to their prayers." Consequently, "God performed many wonders and signs through the apostles" and increased the Church's numbers. "All the believers were united and shared everything."

Because both Old and New Testaments were created for faith communities, they are best understood in that context. While the Bible truly is for all people, it is particularly intended for and meaningful to an assembly of believers.

Abusing the Bible

Unfortunately, however, the Bible has been used to take advantage of, mistreat, and even oppress groups of people for many reasons, one of which is that those in leadership, the powerful, have distorted interpretations that they inflict on others. In reality it probably has less to do with interpretation and more to do with selfish desires. As I mentioned earlier, the proper way to approach scripture is to exegete, that, is to draw meaning out of it. The improper way to approach scripture, which typically leads to oppression, is eisegesis. This is when one imposes one's own meaning into scripture in order to reinforce one's prejudices. I want to share four ways eisegesis has harmed groups of people over the centuries.

Justification of Slavery

In Genesis 9:24-27 we find a scripture that was repeatedly used to justify the transatlantic slave trade, in which millions of Africans were killed.

> When Noah woke up from his wine, he discovered what his youngest son had done to him. He said,
> "Cursed be Canaan:
> the lowest servant
> he will be for his brothers."
> He also said,
> "Bless the LORD,
> the God of Shem;
> Canaan will be his servant.
> May God give space to Japheth;
> he will live in Shem's tents,
> and Canaan will be his servant."

Noah had three sons who were considered to be the fathers of all the nations. Ham is understood, at least from the biblical account, to be the father of those who populated the continent of Africa and parts of Asia. Again we don't know this to be factual. It is the biblical authors' attempt to give an explanation of something, so that they can get to the real heart of the matter, which was the story of Abraham. Anyway, Noah got drunk one night and decided to take off all of his clothes. His son Ham saw him naked and told his brothers. We are supposed to read that as if to say Ham made fun of his father's nakedness. His brothers, on the other hand, did not find humor in it, so they went in and covered their father up without looking at his nakedness. Noah was so upset the next morning when he found out what happened that he cursed Ham's son Canaan. I remember when I first read the story and thought, "Why is Noah getting drunk and taking off all of his clothes as if he took a dare at a college fraternity party?"

Beginning in 1619 in Virginia, when some Europeans wanted free labor, they needed a justification to enslave people. What better text to use than this story? It was a gross misinterpretation of the text for a few reasons. First, Noah did not curse Ham but one of his sons, Canaan. Since Noah cursed Canaan this gave the Hebrews just cause centuries later to invade, conquer, and suppress the land and inhabitants of Canaan. Second, most of the slavery we read about in the Bible is more like what we know as indentured servitude than the wicked institution that caused the deaths of millions and generations of abuse, although such violence did occur. Lastly, to believe that God wanted Africans to be enslaved based on a story in the Hebrew context thousands of years earlier is just plain silly.

Unfair Portrayal of Mary Magdalene

Another way in which the scriptures have been abused is when it comes to Mary Magdalene. We are introduced to her in Luke 8:1-3.

> Soon afterward, Jesus traveled through the cities and villages, preaching and proclaiming the good news of God's kingdom. The Twelve were with him, along with some women who had been healed of evil spirits and sicknesses. Among them were Mary Magdalene (from whom seven demons had been thrown out), Joanna (the wife of Herod's servant Chuza), Susanna, and many others who provided for them out of their resources.

This, along with other passages of scripture, shows us that Jesus had not only male followers but many female followers as well. Some have suggested that even after the resurrection of Jesus Mary Magdalene was a leader in the early Church in Jerusalem.

However, in an effort to thwart the leadership roles that women could play in the Church, Mary Magdalene had to be discredited. The most notable way in which this happened was when sixth-century Pope Gregory I suggested that Mary Magdalene was, in fact, a prostitute. He somehow connected her with the woman, who most likely was a prostitute, who washed Jesus's feet with perfume as described in Luke 7:36-39.

At least two things need to be stated about connecting Mary Magdalene with this so-called "sinner" in order to justify forbidding women from having leadership in the Church. First, the Bible is full of people who did terrible things yet were still used by God. King David killed Uriah in order to marry his wife. Moses killed a man. Saul, who later became Paul, persecuted followers of Jesus. The list goes on and on. The point is that, if God only used sinless people, then no one would be worthy to serve in God's Church.

Second, there is absolutely no evidence that the woman in Luke 7 who is identified as a sinner is Mary Magdalene. Why that connection was made in the first place can only be because of patriarchal arrogance. It is a complete stretch that has led to the Church and world missing out on the great contributions that could have been made by women had not their voices been suppressed. The Gospels are clear that women were deeply involved in the ministry of Jesus and were the ones brave enough to be with Jesus while he agonized on the cross as Matthew 27:55-56 states: "Many women were watching from a distance. They had followed Jesus from Galilee to serve him. Among them were Mary Magdalene, Mary the mother of James and Joseph, and the mother of Zebedee's sons." Regrettably, the misuse of scripture has contributed to the silence of women in the Church.

Promotion of Anti-Semitism

A third way in which the Bible has been abused (there are many other examples) is when it comes to promoting anti-Semitism. The mistreatment of Jewish people for centuries, which continues in some places even today, can be traced back to an eisegesis of certain biblical texts. Matthew 27:24-26 is one such example.

> Pilate saw that he was getting nowhere and that a riot was starting. So he took water and washed his hands in front of the crowd. "I'm innocent of this man's blood," he said. "It's your problem."
>
> All the people replied, "Let his blood be on us and on our children." Then he released Barabbas to them. He had Jesus whipped, then handed him over to be crucified.

This particular scripture has been used to blame the Jewish people for the death of Jesus. I've heard, and perhaps you have as well, someone say, "The Jews killed Jesus."

The reason this is an absurd statement is that it excuses Pontius Pilate from all responsibility. Pilate was the Roman authority in the Judean Province of the Roman Empire. Therefore, if anyone was responsible for Jesus's death he would be at the top of the list. Pilate had to give the okay before Jesus could be executed. The fact that he says that he doesn't want to doesn't exonerate him. It was done under his authority. It would be like a young child asking a parent if they can steal a candy bar from the store. The parent says, "It's not what I want, but if you really want to steal it, you can." The parent is just as responsible as the child, perhaps even more so because the parent is supposed to know better.

Furthermore, to blame an entire group of people for the actions of a few is crazy. The ones who wanted Jesus dead were some of the Jewish religious leaders, not the entire

Jewish people. In fact, some Jewish leaders became followers of Jesus, for example Nicodemus (see John, chapter 3), and during the time of Jesus's execution most people did not even know who Jesus was, so how could they be blamed for his death? It would be like saying that all black men are criminals because of the actions of a few. Well that might be a bad example because in many cases that does happen. The point is that placing the blame for the death of Jesus on an entire group simply does not make sense.

Lastly, the mere notion that the Bible incites anti-Semitism is hilarious, because Jesus of Nazareth was Jewish. To think that the followers of Jesus have mistreated and abused other people because they share the same heritage as Jesus simply doesn't make sense. Not only is Jesus Jewish, but the apostles, other disciples, and many of the first converts to Christianity were Jewish. So how could a religious group that was birthed out of another hold animosity toward that group? The only way or reason that would happen is because of a distorted interpretation of the Bible.

Not Allowing People to Read the Bible for Themselves

Here is another abuse that is often neglected. For around one thousand years no one, other than clergy, was allowed to read the Bible. It is worth mentioning that many people couldn't read or even afford a scroll or book in the first place. These would have been considered a luxury for the wealthy. But I would conclude the reason for everyday people not having access to the Bible was so that the Church could have greater control over them. If the average person did not know what was contained in scripture, they would have to rely completely on clergy to tell them what it said. Moreover, they would have to rely on Church leaders to tell them what God required of them and how to stay out of hell. I contend that it was due to people's fear of spending eternity being tormented in hell (that was the teaching of the period) that the Church was able to dictate the norms of society. This of course, led to serious corruption in the Church. The purpose of this book is to help the average non-clergy person interpret the Bible for themselves.

Another reason why people were not allowed to read the Bible is for fear that they would misunderstand it. That is to say, the Church believed that all average people were capable of was eisegesis. Without the proper training, the average layperson couldn't possibly interpret it accurately. So in order to protect the integrity of scripture the Church forbid the reading of scripture by laity. Regardless of the reason for prohibiting the reading of the Bible, it is easy to see how this could lead to an abuse of power.

Because so many people hold the Bible in such high esteem, sadly it is used to take advantage of others. So whenever we are trying to find meaning in scripture, it is vital that we are mindful of how it has been used to demean and oppress other groups over the centuries. What is the Bible? It is not meant to be a weapon, despite having been used by the powerful to persecute and marginalize others. But it has also been used to inspire, transform, and uplift countless groups and communities. In order for the latter usage to become the norm, we must focus on the common principles and themes that run all throughout the Bible.

Wrapping It All Up

The Bible has been around for thousands of years. Over the centuries there have been a number of different ways in which people have understood the Bible. Regardless of whether people considered it (1) nothing but interesting literature, (2) something that is hard to understand, (3) superstitious nonsense, or (4) the Word of God, the Bible has had a profound impact on the world.

The expansion and growth of Christianity is a result of this important book being copied and translated into a thousand-plus languages. The spread of Christianity has produced numerous schools, hospitals, retirement centers, nonprofit service organizations, and community centers, plus disaster relief and international cooperation of all kinds. In fact, the Bible has played such an important role shaping the Western world that there is even a Museum of the Bible in Washington, D.C. The purpose of the museum is to show the Bible's influence on the world.

In spite of the Bible's influence there are still many people who have questions about it and find it difficult to comprehend. My hope is that by using the scripture within scripture (John 3:16, Romans 5:8), along with the key principles of grace, mercy, love, and forgiveness, one can gain an appreciation and strong grasp of scripture.

Also, the concepts of freedom and liberation or deliverance are extremely important when seeking meaning from the Bible. The notion of liberation permeates the Bible from the Old Testament to the New Testament. We see it on a personal level with the Jubilee laws (all slaves were set free and all property was returned to the original owners) in the book of Leviticus. It is seen on a societal level when the Hebrews were set free from Egyptian bondage in the book of Exodus. Most of all we see it on a spiritual level with the death and resurrection of Jesus. Liberation is being released from some form of oppression so that we can live in freedom as God intended.

This brings us to the most important way of making sense out of scripture, and that is by looking through the lens of the resurrection of Jesus to interpret texts. It is not the end of the story, because the story continues to go on through all of us by the power of the Holy Spirit. However, it is the culmination and summation of everything God was working to accomplish ever since the Fall of Humanity back in the Garden of Eden with Adam and Eve. For Christians the resurrection is the most important event in human history, regardless of whether you approach scripture literally, allegorically, historically, or morally. The resurrection validates everything that Jesus did and taught.

The resurrection is also the foundation of hope, which is available to people of all ages and backgrounds. Hope is not wishful thinking; it is rooted in a confidence that comes from having a relationship with God. Hope says that I always have a chance regardless of my circumstances. Even when we come to the end of our lives on this earth there is hope. And, as Romans 5:5 explains, "This hope doesn't put us to shame, because the love of God has been poured out in our hearts through the Holy Spirit, who has been given to us."

What is the Bible? It is the story of God's unending love in the world that culminates with the resurrection of Jesus, who gives hope and freedom to all.

Who is the Bible for? It is for anyone and everyone of every era and demographic. In short, the Bible is for you!

Study Questions

I. What Is the Bible?

1. What parts of the Bible are easiest for you to understand?
2. How have you understood the term "Word of God"?
3. Do you think it's important for every Christian to have a strong understanding of who wrote the Bible?
4. What did you learn in this chapter?

II. Why Is the Bible Important?

1. What value does the Bible have for your life?
2. What are the essentials of the Christian faith for you?
3. How can you present the Bible to future generations to make it relevant?
4. What did you learn in this chapter?

III. Why Do We Need to Be Saved?

1. What does it mean to be saved?
2. How important is Jesus to the biblical story?
3. Do you think it is important to have proof that Jesus is who he says he is?
4. What did you learn in this chapter?

IV. How Should We Interpret the Bible?

1. What is your favorite translation of the Bible and why?
2. Do you have a method for interpreting the Bible? If so, what is it?
3. How do you deal with some of the disturbing images and stories in the Bible?
4. What did you learn in this chapter?

V. Helpful Tools

1. What are your favorite principles found in the Bible?
2. What are ways we mistreat the poor and practice idolatry today?
3. What are some of your favorite scriptures and why?
4. What did you learn in this chapter?

VI. So What?

1. How would you summarize the life, death, and resurrection of Jesus?
2. In what ways has being part of a faith community helped in your understanding of the Bible?
3. Are there any recent examples of people abusing the Bible?
4. How can we take what we've learned about the Bible and put it into practice?

Endnotes

1. F. L. Cross and E. A. Livingstone, eds., *The Oxford Dictionary of the Christian Church, Third Edition* (New York: Oxford University Press, 1997), 198.

2. James M. Hamilton Jr., *What Is Biblical Theology? A Guide to the Bible's Story, Symbolism, and Patterns* (Wheaton, IL: Crossway, 2014), 16.

3. Michael Lipka, "Why America's 'Nones' Left Religion Behind," Pew Research Center, August 24, 2016 (http://www.pewresearch.org/fact-tank/2016/08/24/why-americas-nones-left-religion-behind/).

4. Robert L. Faherty, "Sacrifice," *Encyclopedia Britannica* online, July 26, 1999 (https://www.britannica.com/topic/sacrifice-religion).

5. Tu Wei-ming, "Confucianism," in *Our Religions*, ed. Arvind Sharma (San Francisco: HarperSanFrancisco, 1993), 141.

6. David Gill, "Socrates and Jesus on Non-Retaliation and Love of Enemies," *Horizons*, vol. 18, no. 2 (Fall 1991) (https://www.cambridge.org/core/journals/horizons/article/socrates-and-jesus-on-nonretaliation-and-love-of-enemies/3C8ECC78DA10F4703D10A260262F4E9A#).

7. Joseph A. Fitzmyer, *The Gospel According to Luke: I-IX*, The Anchor Bible Volume 28 (Garden City, NY: Doubleday, 1989), 59.

8. Robert C. Tannehill, *Luke*, Abingdon New Testament Commentaries (Nashville: Abingdon Press, 1996), 25.

9. Tannehill, 26.

10. Tannehill, 24.

11. Sharon H. Ringe, *Luke*, Westminster Bible Companion (Louisville, KY: Westminster John Knox Press, 1999), 10.

12. Ringe, 9.

13. Ringe, 66.

CPSIA information can be obtained
at www.ICGtesting.com
Printed in the USA
LVHW050000301020
669934LV00006B/322